THE SHALLOW END

Doug Lucie

**The Royal Court Writers Series published by
Methuen Drama in association with
the Royal Court Theatre**

Royal Court Writers Series

First published in Great Britain in the
Royal Court Writers Series in 1997
by Methuen Drama
an imprint of Reed International Books Ltd
Michelin House, 81 Fulham Road, London SW3 6RB
and Auckland, Melbourne, Singapore and Toronto
and distributed in the United States of America
by Heinemann, a division of Reed Elsevier Inc
361 Hanover Street, Portsmouth, New Hampshire
03901 3959
in association with the Royal Court Theatre
St Martin's Lane, London WC2N 4BG

ISBN 0 413 71680 5

A CIP catalogue record for this book is available at the
British Library

Typeset by Wilmaset Ltd, Birkenhead, Wirral
Printed and bound in Great Britain by
Cox & Wyman Ltd, Reading, Berkshire

*The Royal Court
presents*

The Shallow End

by Doug Lucie

*First performance at the
Royal Court Theatre Downstairs, St Martin's Lane 13 February 1997.*

The Royal Court Theatre is financially assisted by the Royal
Borough of Kensington and Chelsea. Recipient of a grant from
the Theatre Restoration Fund & from the Foundation for Sport
& the Arts. The Royal Court's Play Development Programme
is funded by the Audrey Skirball-Kenis Theatre. Supported by
the National Lottery through the Arts Council of England.
Royal Court Registered Charity number 231242.

PRODUCED IN ASSOCIATION WITH
CAMERON MACKINTOSH

AT THOMAS NEAL'S

Principal Sponsor

MERCURY
COMMUNICATIONS

A CABLE & WIRELESS COMPANY

THE FIX
A MUSICAL BY
JOHN DEMPSEY
AND
DANA P. ROWE

SAM MENDES DIRECTS THE TALE OF ONE MAN'S
METEORIC RISE & FALL SET AGAINST THE BACK
DROP OF MODERN AMERICAN POLITICS

WORLD PREMIERE
25 APR - 14 JUNE

4 CORNERS
EXCLUSIVELY PREMIERING THE
BRIGHTEST TALENT OF BRITAIN AND
IRELAND ON A WEST END STAGE

WALES
THIN LANGUAGE

BADFINGER
BY SIMON HARRIS
11-22 MARCH

ENGLAND
IN ASSOCIATION WITH
RNT STUDIO

SUMMER BEGINS
BY DAVID ELDRIDGE
25 MAR - 5 APR

IRELAND
ROUGH MAGIC
THEATRE COMPANY

HALLOWEEN NIGHT
BY DECLAN HUGHES
8 - 19 APRIL

11 MARCH - 19 APRIL

BOX OFFICE:
0171 369 1732

sponsored by
CARLTON

The English Stage Company at the Royal Court Theatre

The English Stage Company was formed to bring serious writing back to the stage. The first Artistic Director, George Devine, wanted to create a vital and popular theatre. He encouraged new writing that explored subjects drawn from contemporary life as well as pursuing European plays and forgotten classics. When John Osborne's **Look Back in Anger** was first produced in 1956, it forced British Theatre into the modern age. In addition to plays by "angry young men", the international repertoire ranged from Brecht to Ionesco, by way of Jean Paul Sartre, Marguerite Duras, Wedekind and Beckett.

The ambition was to discover new work which was challenging, innovative and also of the highest quality, underpinned by the desire to discover a contemporary style of presentation. Early Court writers included Arnold Wesker, John Arden, David Storey, Ann Jellicoe, N F Simpson and Edward Bond. They were followed by David Hare and Howard Brenton, Caryl Churchill, Timberlake Wertenbaker, Robert Holman and Jim Cartwright. Many of their plays are now regarded as modern classics.

Many established playwrights had their early plays produced in the Theatre Upstairs including Anne Devlin, Andrea Dunbar, Sarah Daniels, Jim Cartwright, Clare McIntyre, Winsome Pinnock, Martin Crimp and Phyllis Nagy. Since 1994 there has been a major season of plays by writers new to the Royal Court, many of them first plays, produced in association with the *Royal National Theatre Studio* with sponsorship from *The Jerwood Foundation*. The writers include Joe Penhall, Nick Grosso, Judy Upton, Sarah Kane, Michael Wynne, Judith Johnson, James Stock, Simon Block and Mark Ravenhill. In 1996-97 The Jerwood Foundation sponsored the Jerwood New Playwright season, a series of six plays by Jez Butterwoth and Martin McDonagh (in the Theatre Downstairs), Mark Ravenhill, Ayub Khan-Din, Tamantha Hammerschlag and Jess Walters (in the Theatre Upstairs).

Theatre Upstairs productions have regularly transferred to the Theatre Downstairs, as with Ariel Dorfman's **Death and the Maiden**, Sebastian Barry's **The Steward of Christendom**, a co-production with *Out of Joint*, and Martin McDonagh's **The Beauty Queen Of Leenane,** a co-production with Druid Theatre Company. Some Theatre Upstairs productions have transferred to the West End, most recently with Kevin Elyot's **My Night With Reg** at the Criterion.

1992-1996 have been record-breaking years at the box-office with capacity houses for productions of **Faith Healer**, **Death and the Maiden**, **Six Degrees of Separation**, **King Lear**, **Oleanna**, **Hysteria**, **Cavalcaders**, **The Kitchen**, **The Queen & I**, **The Libertine**, **Simpatico**, **Mojo** and **The Steward of Christendom**.

Death and the Maiden and **Six Degrees of Separation** won the Olivier Award for Best Play in 1992 and 1993 respectively. **Hysteria** won the 1994 Olivier Award for Best Comedy, and also the Writers' Guild Award for Best West End Play. **My Night with Reg** won the 1994 Writers' Guild Award for Best Fringe Play, the Evening Standard Award for Best Comedy, and the 1994 Olivier Award for Best Comedy. Jonathan Harvey won the 1994 Evening Standard Drama Award for Most Promising Playwright, for **Babies**. Sebastian Barry won the 1995 Writers' Guild Award for Best Fringe Play for **The Steward of Christendom** and also the 1995 Lloyds Private Banking Playwright of the Year Award. Jez Butterworth won the 1995 George Devine Award for Most Promising Playwright, the 1995 Writers' Guild New Writer of the Year, the Evening Standard Award for Most Promising Newcomer and the 1995 Olivier Award for Best Comedy for **Mojo**. Phyllis Nagy won the 1995 Writers' Guild Award for Best Regional Play for **Disappeared**. Martin McDonagh won the 1996 George Devine Award for Most Promising Playwright, the 1996 Writers' Guild Best Fringe Play Award, and the 1996 Evening Standard Drama Award for Most promising Newcomer for **The Beauty Queen of Leenane**. The Royal Court won the 1995 Prudential Award for the Theatre, and was the overall winner of the 1995 Prudential Award for the Arts for creativity, excellence, innovation and accessibility. The Royal Court won the 1995 Peter Brook Empty Space Award for innovation and excellence in theatre.

Now in its temporary homes The Duke Of York's and Ambassadors Theatres, during the two-year refurbishment of its Sloane Square theatre, the Royal Court continues to present the best in new work. After four decades the company's aims remain consistent with those established by George Devine. The Royal Court is still a major focus in the country for the production of new work. Scores of plays first seen at the Royal Court are now part of the national and international dramatic repertoire.

Stage Hands Appeal

Royal Court Theatre

A MODEL THEATRE

You've seen the show, read the playtext and eaten the ice-cream - but what to do with all the loose change left over from the evening's entertainment? The Royal Court's 'Model Money Box' may be just the answer. The money box is a replica model of the new-look Royal Court, complete with undercroft cafe, new circle bar balcony and re-shaped auditorium. Notes and coins will be gratefully received.

Many thanks to everyone who has supported the Stage Hands appeal so far. Our goal, to raise over £500,000 from friends and audience members towards the £16 million redevelopment of the Royal Court Theatre, Sloane Square, has already raised £160,000 - a great start.

A special thank you to everyone who is supporting us with covenanted donations: covenants are particularly important because we can claim back the tax a donor has already paid, which increases the value of the donation by *over one third* (at no extra cost to the donor). The same applies to Gift Aid, which adds one third to the value of all single donations of £250 or more. It is vital we make the most of all our donations so if you're able to make a covenanted contribution to the theatre's Stage Hands Appeal please call 0171-930-4253.

BUILDING UPDATE

Both our Lottery grant and partnership funding are hard at work for us now as the Redevelopment in Sloane Square continues apace. With the stripping out-process almost complete, and the stage, seats, fixtures and fittings all removed, we can start to get down to the project's three 'Rs'; Re-structuring, Re-building and Refurbishing.

Hoardings will shortly be going up around the front of the theatre, securing the site and providing building access, which means that the much-loved Royal Court Theatre facade will disappear from view for a while. However, out-of-sight (or should that be site?) is definitely not out-of-mind and a photo display in the Theatre Downstairs lobby will provide building updates as the work progresses.

Stage Hands Appeal

40TH ANNIVERSARY GALA

The Porchester Hall in Queensway, once notorious for its drag balls and Turkish baths, was the venue for the Royal Court's recent 40th Anniversary gala, hosted by The New Yorker and Hugo Boss.

The centrepiece of this glittering evening was a cabaret directed by the Court's Artistic Director, Stephen Daldry, and as the 450 diners laid down their silverware an explosion shook the room and thirty chefs and waitresses from Arnold Wesker's *The Kitchen* burst onto the stage. But it wasn't just the cast from *The Kitchen* and David Storey's *The Changing Room* who provided the entertainment: Jeremy Irons' rendition of a piece from Christopher Hampton's *Savages*, backed by authentic South American musicians, hushed the room; Sloane Square favourites' Kens Cranham and Campbell performed a piece from *Waiting for Godot*; Harriet Walter re-created her role from Timberlake Wertenbaker's *Three Birds Alighting on a Field*, offering a hilarious portrait of the socialite finding salvation through art; and Stephen Fry delivered PG Wodehouse's wonderful poem, *The Audience at the Court Theatre*.

Famous faces including Melvyn Bragg, Nigel Hawthorne, Helen Mirren, Ruby Wax, Salman Rushdie, Mick Jagger, Jerry Hall and Vanessa Redgrave were thrilled by the theatrical magic of the evening and the money raised by the gala will play an important part in getting the redevelopment work in Sloane Square off the ground.

TAKE YOUR SEATS

There will be almost 400 new seats in the refurbished Theatre Downstairs and over 60 in the Theatre Upstairs - all of which are offered 'for sale'. Not only will the seats in the Theatre Downstairs have the printed name of the seat's 'owner', they will also bear the owner's *signature*. Seats may be bought on behalf of children and grandchildren and can be signed by the children themselves. Companies are also eligible to take part in the scheme and their business logos will printed on the plaques. For details of the 'Take A Seat' scheme please call 0171-930-4253.

STAGE HANDS T-SHIRTS

Stage Hands T-shirts are now on sale at the Bookshop in the Theatre Downstairs and in the Bar at the Theatre Upstairs, price £10.

For futher details about Stage Hands and the Redevelopment please call the Development Office on 0171-930-4253

The Shallow End

by Doug Lucie

Editorial

Slater	Julia Ford
Kirk	Tony Doyle
Drummond	Nicholas Day
Snape	James Aubrey

Sport, Showbiz, Comment

Budge	David Cardy
Whistler	Trevor Cooper
Coleman	John Nettleton
Percy	Denys Hawthorne
Waiter	Paul Williams
Viggers	Theo Fraser Steele
Waitress	Angie Alderman

Home and Politics

Toop	Alan David
Brennan	Alexander Hanson
Alison Toop	Jane Asher
Drummond	Nicholas Day

Foreign

Kirk	Tony Doyle
Drummond	Nicholas Day
Rees	Nigel Terry
Fleming	Stan Pretty

Director	Robin Lefevre
Designer	Robin Don
Lighting Designer	Mick Hughes
Sound Designer	Paul Arditti
Production Manager	Edwyn Wilson
Stage Manager	Martin Christopher
Deputy Stage Manager	Sophie Gabszewicz
Assistant Stage Manager	Debbie Green
Student Assistant Stage Manager	Ian Micheals
Costume Supervisor	Jennifer Cook
Scenery	PL Parsons
Flown Photographic Images	Scanachrome Ltd.
Flying Consultants	Stage Surgeons Ltd.

The Royal Court would like to thank the following for their help with this production: Auditorium redesign by Ultz; auditorium ceiling constructed by Stage Surgeons Ltd. (0171 237 2765), rigged and suspended by Vertigo Rigging Ltd.; Alfred Dunhill Ltd for cigarette lighters; Durex Condoms, Hubbard Refridgeration Ltd, suppliers of Scotsman Ice machines 01473 890129; Kings Cross Snooker Club; Nat West Card Services; Theatre Royal Stratford East; W.A Ingram Associates Ltd for Zippo Lighters; Veuve Clicquot (UK) Ltd for stage champagne; Wardrobe care by Persil and Comfort courtesy of Lever Brothers Ltd, refrigerators by Electrolux and Philips Major Appliances Ltd.; kettles for rehearsals by Morphy Richards; video for casting purposes by Hitachi; backstage coffee machine by West 9; furniture by Knoll International; freezer for backstage use supplied by Zanussi Ltd 'Now that's a good idea.' Hair styling by Carole at Moreno, 2 Holbein Place, Sloane Square 0171- 730- 0211; Closed circuit TV cameras and monitors by Mitsubishi UK Ltd. Natural spring water from Wye Spring Water, 149 Sloane Street, London SW1, tel. 0171-730 6977. Overhead projector from W.H. Smith; Sanyo U.K for the backstage microwave.

Doug Lucie (writer)
At the Royal Court:
Doing the Business.
Other theatre work includes:
The New Garbo (Hull Truck);
Heroes (Edinburgh Festival);
Strangers in the Night (New End
Theatre); Hard Feelings (Oxford
Playhouse, Bush Theatre); Key
to the World (Paines Plough,
Lyric Hammersmith); Progress
(Bush Theatre, Lyric
Hammersmith and productions
in Connecticut, New York,
Germany and Scandinavia.
Winner Plays and Players Most
Promising Playwright); Fashion
(RSC, Leicester Haymarket,
Tricycle and productions in
Holland and Israel; Winner
Time Out Award); Grace
(Hampstead and USA); Gaucho
(Hampstead).
Work for television includes:
Hard Feelings, A Class of His
Own, Funseekers, Headhunters.

Angie Alderman
Theatre includes: Eve (Tristan
Bates Theatre); Shoe Shop of
Desire (Red Room); Della
Morte (Barons Court); Mystery
at Greenfingers (Watermans);
Womberang (Bellairs Theatre);
Macbeth (Hong Kong Cultural
Centre and tour); Waking Up
(Arts Festival Hong Kong);
West, Look Back in Anger
(Studio Theatre, Hong Kong).
Television includes: Soldier
Soldier, Ginger Gap, Junior
Junction, Boomerang, Eye-on-
Hong-Kong.

Paul Arditti
(sound design)
For the Royal Court work
includes: The One You Love,
Shopping and F***ing (and Out
of Joint); The Lights, The
Thickness of Skin, Sweetheart,
Bruises, Pale Horse, The
Changing Room, Hysteria, Rat
in the Skull (Royal Court
Classics), The Steward of

Christendom (and Out of Joint),
Mojo, Simpatico, The Strip,
Blasted, Peaches, Some Voices,
Thyestes, My Night with Reg,
The Kitchen, Search and
Destroy. Other theatre sound
design includes: As You Like It
(RSC); Tartuffe (Manchester
Royal Exchange); The
Threepenny Opera (Donmar
Warehouse); Hamlet (Gielgud);
Piaf (Piccadilly); St. Joan
(Strand & Sydney Opera
House); The Trackers of
Oxyrhynchus (RNT); The Gift
of the Gorgon (RSC); Orpheus
Descending (Theatre Royal,
Haymarket & Broadway); The
Merchant of Venice (Phoenix &
Broadway); A Streetcar Named
Desire (Bristol Old Vic);
Matador (Queens); The Rose
Tattoo (Playhouse); Becket,
Cyrano de Bergerac (Theatre
Royal, Haymarket); Travesties
(Savoy); Four Baboons Adoring
the Sun (Lincoln Center, 1992
Drama Desk Award).
Opera includes: Gawain, Arianna
(ROH); The Death of Moses
(Royal Albert Hall).
Television includes:
The Camomile Lawn.

Jane Asher
For the Royal Court: The
Philanthropist (also Mayfair
and Broadway), Treats (and
Mayfair), Look Back in Anger
(and Criterion).
Other theatre includes: Romeo
and Juliet, Measure for Measure
(Bristol Old Vic and Broadway);
Strawberry Fields, The School
for Scandal (RNT); Who's Life
is it Anyway? (Mermaid and
Savoy); Peter Pan (Shaftesbury);
Henceforward (Globe); Making
it Better (Hampstead and
Criterion).
Television includes: The Choir,
Murder Most Horrid, Wish Me
Luck, The Mistress, Bright
Smiler, East Lynne, A Voyage
Round My Father, Love is Old

Love is New, Brideshead
Revisited, The Mill on the
Floss.
Film includes: Closing
Numbers, Paris by Night,
Dream Child, Success is the
Best Revenge, Runners, Henry
VIII and his Wives, Deep End,
Alfie, Greengage Summer.

James Aubrey
For the Royal Court: Bird Child,
Amy and the Price of Cotton,
Millennium, Magnificence,
Loot.
Other theatre includes: two and a
half years at the Citizens
Theatre, Glasgow; Measure for
Measure, The Tempest, A Force
Might Come (RSC); Isle of
Children (Cort Theatre, New
York); Dr Faustus (Fortune);
City Sugar (Comedy); King
Lear, The Rivals (Old Vic);
Marino Faliero (Young Vic);
The Glass Menagerie (Shaw);
Streamers (Roundhouse);
Hitting Town (Bush); The Film
Society, Bloody Poetry
(Hampstead); The Possessed
(Almeida); Macbeth, Who's
Life is it Anyway? (Cambridge
Theatre Company tour of India);
Tamburlaine the Great, Twelfth
Night (Edinburgh Festival); Exit
the King (Lyric Hammersmith);
repertory seasons at Liverpool,
Birmingham and Manchester.
Television includes: Bouquet of
Barbed Wire, Another Bouquet,
The Men's Room, The Choir,
The Last Place on Earth, Full
Stretch, Thin Air, The
Possessed, Silent Witness,
Rockliffe's Babies, Lytton's
Diary, Harry, Return of the
Saint, The Glass Menagerie,
Casualty, The Bill, The
Cleopatras, Inspector Morse,
Lovejoy, Selling Hitler, Danton's
Death, Saint Joan, Emmerdale,
Brookside, Van der Valk,
Minder, The Sweeney,
Infidelities, A Fatal Inversion,
The Final Frame, The Mountain

and the Molehill, Tales of the Unexpected, Mission Eureka. Film includes: Lord of the Flies, Forever Young, Buddy's Song, Cry Freedom, The American Way, Riders of the Storm, The Hunger, A Demon in My View, The Great Rock and Roll Swindle, Terror, Home Before Midnight, Galileo.

David Cardy

For the Royal Court: No End of Blame. Other theatre includes: Pickwick (Oxford Apollo, Chichester, Sadlers Wells and tour); The Tempest, The Comedy of Errors, Love's Labour's Lost, A Midsummer Night's Dream (Open Air Theatre, Regents Park); The Comedians (Belgrade); Penny Blue (Greenwich); On the Razzle, Sinbad's Arabian Nights, Three Musketeers, Fertility Dance (Nuffield); Baby Love (Leatherhead, Nuffield); Double Take (Minerva Studio, Chichester); Coriolanus (Chichester); Twelfth Night (Peter Hall Company); As You Like It (Old Vic): Men in Suits (Boulevard); A Chorus of Disapproval (Lyric); On the Edge (Hampstead); One for the Road (national tour); Sunday Morning, Command or Promise, True Dare Kiss, Up for None (RNT); The Rocky Horror Show (Italian tour); Progress (Bush); Can't Pay? Won't Pay! (Criterion); Mephisto (Roundhouse). Television includes: The Bill, Absolutely Fabulous, Chef, Kavangh, Jo Brand Through the Cakehole, Eastenders, Colin Corleone, Safe, The New Statesman, Queen of the Wild Frontier, Fool's Gold, The Crying Game, The Chief, Stay Lucky, London's Burning, Nightingales, Birds of a Feather, Vote for Them, Hard Cases,

Campaign, Cats Eyes, Under the Hammer, Honeymoon, Crown Court, Broken Glass, Hazell, Rock Follies. Film includes: Winds of War, The Keep, Xtro, Little Dorritt, Prick Up Your Ears, Three Steps to Heaven, Monk Dawson.

Trevor Cooper

For the Royal Court: Live Like Pigs. Other theatre includes: Andy Capp (Royal Exchange, Aldwych); Having a Ball (Theatre Royal York); Jesus Christ Superstar (York); The Ragged Trousered Philanthropist (Half Moon Theatre); Hamlet, Cymbeline, Twelfth Night, Winding the Ball, Julius Caesar, Absurd Person Singular (Royal Exchange); The Hired Man (Nuffield); Great Expectations; Court in the Act (Phoenix); The Three Musketeers (Bristol Old Vic); Accidental Death of an Anarchist (RNT); Strange Snow (Teatro Technics); Zenobia (RSC); According to Hoyle (Hampstead). Television includes: Underbelly, A Wanted Man, Redemption, Baal, Star Cops, Framed, Strife, Casualty, The Singing Detective, A Very Peculiar Practice, Mr Pye, Dr Who, Diana, Smiley's People, The Merchant of Venice, Fatal Spring, Making Out, Bergerac, Mother Love, The Bill, Stay Lucky, Boon, Lovejoy, Poirot, Minder, Love Hurts, Drop the Dead Donkey, Perfect Scoundrels, An Ungentlemanly Act, Gallowglass, Frank Stubbs Promotes, Our Friends in the North, Loved Up, A Very Open Prison, Out of the Blue, Ivanhoe, Perfect State, Insiders. Film includes: Nocturne, The Woman in Black, Drowning by Numbers, Whistle Blower, Billy the Kidd and the Green Baize Vampire, Moonlighting, Final

Warning, Wuthering Heights, The Silent Touch, Century.

Alan David

For the Royal Court: Karate Billy Comes Home, Apples, Road, Panic, The Genius, Rita Sue and Bob Too. Other theatre includes: Volpone, Under Milk Wood, The Merry Wives of Windsor, The School for Scandal (RNT); In the Company of Men, Nicholas Nickleby, As You Like It, Lorenzaccio Story, 'Tis Pity She's a Whore, Dance of Death (RSC). Television includes: A Perfect State, Hetty Wainthropp, Reggie Perrin, Only You, The Brittas Empire, In Suspicious Circumstances, Casualty, The Detectives, Preston Front, Chiller, Heartbeat, Little Bit of Lippy, Devil's Advocate, Cracker, Maigret, Tour of the Western Isles, Gone to the Dogs, Inspector Morse, Headhunters, Thicker than Water, The Vet, Peak Practice, Lovejoy, Shoestring, Honey for Tea, Chris Cross, Virtual Murder, Sleepers, Making Out, There Comes a Time, Foxy Lady, Circe Complex, Coronation Street, The Squirrels, Sam.

Nicholas Day

Theatre includes: The Merchant of Venice (Queens Theatre, Hornchurch); Absurd Person Singular, Abigail's Party (Churchill, Bromley); Taking Steps, I Do Not Like Thee, Dr Fell (Palace, Watford); Abigail's Party (Windsor); A Small Family Business (Coliseum, Oldham); High Fidelity, The Norman Conquests (Triumph tour); The Taming of the Shrew (British Actors Theatre Company); The Beaux Stratagem, Murmuring Judges, Absence of War, Johnny on a Spot, Dealer's Choice

(RNT); Racing Demon (RNT/ Los Angeles); Close Encounters (The Almost Free Theatre); Crucifer of Blood (Haymarket); Death and the Devil (Bush); Love on the Plastic (Half Moon); Ask for the Moon (Hampstead); Night Must Fall (Greenwich); The Game's Rule (Watermans).
Television includes: Ripping Yarns, Grandad, Cribb, Grundy, Chintz, Crown Court, Can We Get on Now Please, Madge, It Takes a Worried Man, A Still Small Shout, Heart Attack Hotel, Harry's Game, The Citadel, Call Me Mister, Saracen, Shelley, Bounder, Full House, CATS Eyes, Up the Elephant and Round the Castle, Bust, Sixpenny Steps, Full House, After the War, Vote for Them, Trouble in Mind, Drop the Dead Donkey, Kappattoo II, Kavanagh QC, The Bill.
Film includes: Mountbatten the Last Viceroy, The Human Bomb.

Robin Don (designer)
For the Royal Court:
The Knocky.
Other theatre includes: Picasso's Four Little Girls and most of the Marowitz Shakespeares, Sherlock's Last Case, Artaud at Rodez, Anatol (Open Space); Bartholomew Fair (Roundhouse); When I Was a Girl I Used To Scream and Shout (Whitehall, Bush and Lyceum Edinburgh); Kiss of the Spiderwoman, The Marshalling Yard, Darwin's Flood, Buried Treasure (Bush); Beautiful Thing (Bush, Donmar and Duke of York's); The Water Engine, Spookhouse (Hampstead); The Ticket of Leave Man (RNT); Twelfth Night, Les Enfants du Paradis (RSC); A Walk in the Woods (Comedy); The Rocky Horror Show (Piccadilly and 21st Birthday tour); The Winter Guest (West Yorkshire Playhouse and Almeida); A Perfect Ganesh (West Yorkshire Playhouse); Fool for Love (Donmar).
Design for opera and ballet includes: Les Mamelles de Tireslas (Opera North and ENO); Mary Queen of Scots (Scottish Opera); Macbeth (Santiago de Chile and Scottish Ballet); A Midsummer Night's Dream (Aldeburgh Festival and ROH); The Midsummer Marriage (San Francisco Opera); Don Quichotte (New York City Opera); Eugene Onegin (Aldeburgh Festival, Rejkajavik, San Diego, San Francisco, Toronto); Tamerlano (Opera de Lyon); Peter Grimes, Carmen, La Forza del Destino (Sydney Opera House).
Robin's design for Eugene Onegin at the Aldeburgh Festival was part of the British entry which won the Golden Troika award at the Prague Quadrienalle. For The Winter Guest at West Yorkshire Playhouse, he won the 1995 TMA and Martini Rossi Regional Theatre Award for Best Designer. In February 1996 he was presented with Designer of the Year Award by the Critics Circle.

Tony Doyle
For the Royal Court:
Rat in the Skull, Cavalcaders (and Abbey).
Other theatre includes: The Gigli Concert (Abbey and Almeida); Too Late for Logic (Abbey); Old Year's Eve (RSC); Translations (Hampstead and RNT); Shadow of a Gunman (Crucible Sheffield); John Bull's Other Island, Da (Greenwich); The Plough and the Stars (RNT); The Birthday Party (Shaw);Mr Joyce is Leaving Paris (Dublin Festival and the King's Head).
Television includes: Ballykissangel, Castles, Band of Gold, Between the Lines, A Murder in Eden, Taggart, Headhunters, You Me and Marley, Rumpole of the Bailey, Firm Friends, Stay Lucky, Rides, Underbelly, Arise and Go Now, Children of the North, The Hen House, Here is the News, Shadow of the Noose, The Contractor, The Nightwatch, Crossfire, Vanity Fair, The Venus de Milo Instead, Bookmark - Samuel Beckett, Slip Up, Frankie and Johnny, McCabes Wall, My Brother Jonathan, The Long March, A Woman Calling, The Waiting War, Two Weeks in Winter, Macbeth, Moving on the Edge, Soft Targets, After the Party, Beloved Enemy, Red Roses for Me, 1990, King of the Castle, Who Bombed Birmingham, The Treaty, Lovers of the Lake, Great Writers: James Joyce, South Bank Show : George Higgins.
Film includes: I Went Down, Circle of Friends, Damage, Secret Friends, Devil's Paradise, Eat the Peach, Walter, Who Dares Wins, Loophole.

Julia Ford
For the Royal Court:
Some Singing Blood.
Other theatre includes: Now You Know (Hampstead); The Lodger (Royal Exchange and Hampstead); Chinese Wolf (Bush Theatre); Hamlet (Riverside Studios and tour); A Doll's House, Who's Afraid of Virginia Woolf? (Wolsey Theatre, Ipswich); Pool of Bethesda (Orange Tree); Piano, The Crucible, Yerma, School for Wives (RNT); The Blood of Others (RNT Studio); Jumping the Rug (RSC/Almeida Festival); Duchess of Malfi, Two Wheel Tricycle, The Mother, A Midsummer Night's

Dream (Contact Theatre, Manchester); Knickers (Bristol Old Vic); Henry IV, King John, Much Ado About Nothing (RSC); Venus and Adonis (Almeida); Accrington Pals, Tartuffe, The Railway Children, Touched (Oldham Coliseum). Television includes: Insiders, Accused, Eight Hours from Paris, The Bill, Strike Force, Medics, Blood and Fire, Peak Practice, The Healer, In Suspicious Circumstances, A Skirt Through History, Casualty, A Fatal Inversion, Bergerac, The Continental, The Ritz, The Practice.

Theo Fraser Steele
Theatre includes: A Week with Tony (Finborough); Bacillus (The Red Room); Amphitryon (Gate); Tamburlaine the Great (RSC). Television includes: Casualty. Film includes: Her Majesty Mrs Brown, When in London, Waterland.

Alexander Hanson
Theatre includes: The Memory of Water (Hampstead); Sunset Boulevard (Adelphi); Arcadia (Haymarket); Intimate Exchanges (Northcott); Time of My Life (national tour); Aspects of Love (Prince of Wales); Valentine's Day (Globe); Oscar (The Old Fire Station); Playing With Fire (Orange Tree); Matador (Queens); Young Apollo (Thorndike); Hand Over Fist (Watermill); A Little Night Music (Chichester and Piccadilly); The Royal Baccarat Scandal, Hay Fever, Translations, Mr Puntila and His Man Matti, Game of Love and Chance, Fire Raisers, An Ideal Husband, A Man for All Seasons, Robert and Elizabeth (Chichester); Brel (Donmar); An Ideal Husband, Tea in a

China Cup, Tom Jones (Redgrave). Television includes: Peak Practice, Doctor Finlay, Casualty, Ffizz, Fellow Traveller, Museums of Madness, The Black Candle, Taking the Floor, Boon, The Chief, Six Characters in Search of an Author.

Denys Hawthorne
For the Royal Court: The Terrible Voice of Satan, Jacque. Other theatre includes: Who's Life is it Anyway?, Chips With Everything, As You Like It, Weekend Break, A Man for All Seasons (Birmingham Rep); Case of the Frightened Lady, Tartuffe (Churchill, Bromley); The Scythe and the Sunset, The Seagull (Irish Theatre Company); Duet for One (Theatre Royal, Plymouth); Hidden Curriculum (Lyric, Belfast); Stuffing It (Tricycle); Season's Greetings (Watford); Mumbo Jumbo (Royal Exchange Manchester, Lyric Hammersmith); Night Must Fall (Greenwich); Exit and Entrance (Abbey Theatre Studio and Donmar); Busman's Honeymoon (Lyric Hammersmith); Uncle Vanya (Bristol Old Vic); Henry IV Part I, Henry IV Part II, Oedipus Rex, Oedipus Colonus, Romeo and Juliet, Artists and Admirers, Macbeth (RSC); Someone to Watch Over Me (Abbey, Dublin); The Earl Bishop (Lyric Theatre, Belfast); Julius Ceasar, Absurd Person Singular (Royal Exchange). Television includes: Within These Walls, Lloyd George, Strumpet City, Red Roses for Me, Roses From Dublin, Harry's Game, The Long March, Rumpole of the Bailey, An Englishman Abroad, Crossfire, This is David Lander,

Chelworth, Poirot, Hannay, Capital City, The Englishman's Wife, Inspector Morse, Little Green Men, William's War, Moon and Son, Breed of Heroes, The Bill, Dangerfield, Father Ted, Have Your Cake and Eat It. Film includes: Human Factor, A Private Function, Mountbatten, Blanc de Chine, Jack the Ripper, The Russia House, House of Spirits, In the Name of the Father, Emma, Monk Dawson.

Mick Hughes
(lighting design) For the Royal Court: Ashes to Ashes. Other recent lighting design for theatre includes: The Revenger's Comedies, Body Language, Wildest Dreams, Othello, Taking Sides, One Over the Eight, Time of My Life, Communicating Doors (Stephen Joseph Theatre); The Pinter Season, Molly Sweeney (Gate Theatre, Dublin); Lizzie Finn (Abbey Theatre, Dublin); Mrs Warren's Profession, Death of a Salesman, The Caretaker, The Trojan War Will Not Take Place, A Little Hotel on the Side, A Chorus of Disapproval, Tons of Money, A View from the Bridge, A Small Family Business, 'Tis Pity She's a Whore, Fuente Ovejuna, The March on Russia, Man Beast and Virtue, Invisible Friends, Angels in America, The Rise and Fall of Little Voice, Square Rounds, Stages, Mr A's Amazing Maze Plays, Sweeney Todd, The Devil's Disciple, Dealer's Choice (RNT); Passion Play, The Danton Affair, Wildest Dream (RSC); The Cherry Orchard (Aldwych); Don't Dress for Dinner (Duchess); The Hot House (Comedy); Taking Sides (Criterion): By Jeeves (Duke of York's). Lighting design for opera

includes: The Wexford Festival 1982-1985; Don Pasquale, Mahagonny (ENO).

Mick directed 40 plays for Worcester Rep from 1967 to 1972, and lit all the plays at the Chichester Festival Theatre from 1966 to 1969, and from 1974 to 1979. From 1978 to 1982 he was Lighting Consultant for the Hong Kong Arts Festival.

In 1986 Mick won the Harvey Award in Dublin, for Innocence.

Robin Lefevre (director)
For the Royal Court: Cavalcaders (and Abbey, Dublin).

Other theatre includes: Then and Now, Threads, Writer's Cramp, On the Edge, Fall, Bodies, Spookhouse, According to Hoyle (Hampstead) Aristocrats (Hampstead, Manhattan Theatre Club. Winner Evening Standard Award for Best Play 1988, New York Drama Critics Award for Best Play, Nomination Drama Desk Award for Best Director); Valued Friends (Hampstead and Connecticut); Someone Who'll Watch Over Me (Hampstead, Vaudeville and Broadway); Outside Edge (Queens); Rocket to the Moon, The Country Girl (Apollo); The Big Knife (Albery); Are You Lonesome Tonight? (Evening Standard Award for Best Musical 1985); The New Revue, The Entertainer (Shaftesbury); Candy Kisses, The Number of the Beast, A Handful of Stars, Poor Beast in the Rain (Bush); Some of My Best Friends are Husbands (Leicester Haymarket and tour); When We Are Married (RNT) Richard II (Young Vic); The Rocky Horror Show (Piccadilly); The Curse of the Starving Classes (RSC): The Wexford Trilogy (Bush, Wexford, Dublin); Private Lives (Gate, Dublin); On the Ledge (RNT, Nottingham Playhouse);

The Bird Sanctuary, Translations (Abbey, Dublin); Buried Treasure (Lyric, Hammersmith).

John Nettleton
For the Royal Court: The Good Woman of Setzuan.

Other theatre includes: Camino Real (Phoenix); A Passage to India (Comedy); Becket, The Lower Depths, The Devils, Troilus and Cressida, The Representative, A Midsummer Night's Dream, Afore Night Come, Henry V, Coriolanus, The Hollow Crown (RSC); Rosmersholm (Greenwich); Hamlet, Antony and Cleopatra (Old Vic and Mid-East tour); As You Like It (U.S/Canada tour); Then and Now (Hampstead); Anyone for Denis? (Whitehall); When the Wind Blows (National tour); Tamburlaine, The School for Scandal, The Wind in the Willows (RNT); The Importance of Being Earnest (English Touring Company); The Woman in Black (Fortune and Tivoli, Dublin).

Television includes: Elizabeth R, The Country Wife, The Flame Trees of Thika, Upstairs Downstairs, Brideshead Revisited, A Perfect Spy, East of Ipswich, The Citadel, The Tempest, Strife, Victoria Wood Show, Rumpole of the Bailey, Circles of Deceit, Yes Minister, Yes Prime Minister.

Film includes: A Man for All Seasons, And Soon the Darkness, Burning Secret, American Friends.

Stan Pretty
Theatre includes: The Rover, Romeo and Juliet, Macbeth, Richard II, The Balcony (RSC); Waste, Joseph and the Amazing Technicolor Dreamcoat, Toad of Toad Hall (West End); A Midsummer Night's Dream (Regents Park); Twelfth Night (Ludlow Festival); The Birthday

Party (Citizens Glasgow and tour): Julius Caesar (tour); The Silver King (Swan, Stratford); The Wild Duck, Travelling North (Lyric Hammersmith); The Shop Assistant (Kings Head); The Diary of Anne Frank (Haymarket, Basingstoke); 'Allo 'Allo (Australian tour); Barefoot in the Park (Germany); Poetry Recitals tour.

Television includes: Minder, Bergerac, Dempsey and Makepiece, Boon, Jenny's War.

Film includes: Leon the Pig Farmer, Great Moments in Aviation.

Radio: Short Story (Radio Four), Interview Documentary producer.

He is co-founder of The Travelling Light Shakespeare Company, and co-author, with Jonathan Milton, of the company's two shows Burbage and the Bard and A Cry of Players, which have played throughout Britain and abroad over the past six years.

Nigel Terry
Theatre includes: season/touring with: Out of Joint, Joint Stock, the Royal Court, Cheek by Jowl, Sheffield, Manchester, Leeds, RNT and RSC.

Television includes: Resort to Murder, The Mushroom Picker The Orchid House, Jackanory, The Ebb Tide.

Films include: Caravaggio, Edward II, Last of England, War Requiem, Blue (all for Derek Jarman).

Paul Williams
This is Paul's professional stage debut.

Share more fully in the life of the Royal Court by joining our supporters and investing in New Theatre

Call: 0171-930-4253

Many thanks to all our supporters for their vital and on-going commitment

TRUSTS AND FOUNDATIONS
The Baring Foundation
The Campden Charities
John Cass's Foundation
The Chase Charity
The Esmeé Fairbairn
 Charitable Trust
The Robert Gavron
 Charitable Trust
Paul Hamlyn Foundation
The Jerwood Foundation
The John Lyons' Charity
The Mercers' Charitable
 Foundation
The Prince's Trust
Peggy Ramsay Foundation
The Rayne Foundation
The Lord Sainsbury
Foundation for Sport
 & the Arts
The Wates Foundation

SPONSORS
AT&T
Barclays Bank
Hugo Boss
Brunswick PR Ltd
Citibank
The Evening Standard
The Granada Group Plc
John Lewis Partnership
Marks & Spencer Plc
The New Yorker

Prudential Corporation Plc
W H Smith

CORPORATE PATRONS
Advanpress
Associated Newspapers Ltd
Bunzl Plc
Citigate Communications
Criterion Productions Plc
Deloitte & Touche
Dibb Lupton Broomhead
Homevale Ltd
Laporte Plc
Lazard Brothers & Co., Ltd
Lex Service Plc
The Mirror Group Plc
New Penny Productions Ltd
News Corporation Ltd
Noel Gay Artists Hamilton
 Asper Management
A T Poeton & Son Ltd
The Simkins Partnership
Simons Muirhead and
 Burton

PATRONS
Sir Christopher Bland
Greg Dyke
Spencer & Calla Fleischer
Barbara Minto
Greville Poke
Richard Pulford
Sir George Russell
Richard Wilson

ASSOCIATES
Nicholas A Fraser
Patricia Marmont

BENEFACTORS
Mr & Mrs Gerry Acher
David H. Adams
Bill Andrewes
Batia Asher
Elaine Attias
Angela Bernstein
Jeremy Bond
Julia Brodie
Julian Brookstone
Guy Chapman
Carole & Neville Conrad
Conway van Gelder
Coppard Fletcher & Co.
Lisa Crawford Irwin
Curtis Brown Ltd
Louise & Brian Cuzner
Allan Davis
Robert Dufton
Robyn Durie

Gill Fitzhugh
Kim Fletcher & Sarah Sands
Winston Fletcher
Norman Gerard
Henny Gestetner OBE
Jules Goddard
Carolyn Goldbart
Rocky Gottlieb
Stephen Gottlieb
Frank & Judy Grace
Jan Harris
Angela Heylin
Andre Hoffman
Chris Hopson
Jane How & Richard Durden
Institute of Practitioners
in Advertising
International Creative
Management
Jarvis Hotels
Peter Jones
Sahra Lese
Judy Lever
Lady Lever
Pat Morton
Gerard Norman
Michael Orr
Sir Eric Parker
Lynne Pemberton
Carol Rayman
Angharad Rees
B J & Rosemary Reynolds
John Sandoe (Books) Ltd
Scott Tallon Walker
Nicholas Selmes
Maria Shammas
Lord Sheppard
Sue Stapely
Dr Gordon Taylor
Tomkins Plc
Eric Walters
A P Watt Ltd
Sue Weaver, The Sloane
 Club
Nick Wilkinson

AMERICAN FRIENDS
Patrons
Miriam Blenstock
Tina Brown
Caroline Graham
Richard & Marcia Grand
Ann & Mick Jones
Maurie Perl
Rhonda Sherman
Members
Monica Gerard-Sharp
Linda S. Lese
Enid W. Morse
Paul & Daisy Soros

Characters

Section One

Malcolm Kirk . . . *Late forties. Editor.*
Nikki Slater . . . *Early thirties. Columnist and author.*
Rob Drummond . . . *Forty. Deputy Editor.*
Ray Snape . . . *Late thirties. Features Editor.*

Section Two

Sir Bob Coleman . . . *Sixties. Former Thatcher aide who now writes a Sunday column for the paper.*
Percy Wadsworth . . . *Sixties. Another former Thatcher aide cum journalist.*
Waiter . . . *Twenty. A young man stuck in a McJob.*
Mike Viggers . . . *Twenties. Style and showbiz journalist.*
Waitress . . . *Twenties.*
Budge . . . *Twenties. Style and showbiz journalist.*
Dave Whistler . . . *Early forties. Football writer.*

Section Three

Stephen Toop . . . *Forties. Political Editor.*
Alison Toop . . . *Forties. Stephen's wife.*
Peter Brennan . . . *Thirties. Political correspondent.*
Rob Drummond . . . *As above.*

Section Four

Malcolm Kirk . . . *As above.*
Rob Drummond . . . *As above.*
Harry Rees . . . *Fiftyish. Foreign correspondent.*
Bryan Fleming . . . *Fiftyish. Chief Executive, Internews.*

The play takes place through one afternoon at the wedding of the daughter of an unnamed media mogul, whose company, Internews, is the biggest of its kind in the world. It controls newspapers on all the continents, satellite television, publishing houses and film and TV companies. The setting is a large house deep in the country which has been hired for the occasion. Most of the characters are journalists on an unnamed Sunday paper, which has been of the centre-left until being bought by Internews six months previously. They have all been ferried to the wedding in a fleet of executive buses. All the male characters, except for the waiter, Whistler and Rees, wear morning suits.

Section One

The trophy room of a big country house. Darkness. A shaft of light as the door is opened and a man and a woman come in. The man fumbles for the light switch. The light comes on, revealing **Kirk** *and* **Slater**. *He wears a morning suit, she wears a very smart jacket over a black micro dress. She stands in the doorway as he turns on a table lamp and smiles at her.*

Kirk   Have a seat. (*She saunters across to an armchair.*)

Slater   What the fuck is this?

Kirk   It's the trophy room.

Slater   Yeah? (*She sits.*) Bit premature, aren't we?

Kirk   Drummond arranged it. Security have this part of the house off-limits.

Slater   So we won't be disturbed.

Kirk   Quite. (*Beat.*) Champagne?

Slater   Lovely. (*He goes to the table where there is a bottle of champagne in an ice bucket. He starts uncorking it.*) D'you know, I saw some prick guzzling it out of the bottle earlier.

Kirk   Ah, well . . .

Slater   What's the point of giving these people something with a bit of class if they're going to miss the point so stupidly every time?

Kirk   Sadly, not everybody can acquire taste, despite our best efforts.

Slater   And the women . . . I've never seen so much Armani worn so wrong. (*Beat.*)

Kirk   -Ly.

Slater   Eh?

Kirk   Wrong-ly. It's an adverb.

Slater   Is that like a split infinity? (*He laughs.*) I mean, you don't splash out on Armani and then wrap it round a sack of spuds. It's like cellulite city out there. (*He pops the champagne cork and pours.*)

Kirk   I think the ladies look very stylish.

Slater   'Ish' is right. I did spot one who knew how to wear it. Long blonde hair, nice tits . . .

Kirk   I must have missed her.

Slater   I thought, there's one person here today that I could happily fuck, and I can't get near her for smeggy blokes in hired suits. (*He hands her a glass.*) Cheers. (*She clinks his glass.*)

Kirk   Cheers. (*Beat. They drink.*) Is that speaking metaphorically, or. . . ?

Slater   Or what? (*Beat.*)

Kirk   The young lady with the long blonde hair . . .

Slater   And the nice tits. Go on, say it.

Kirk   I, uh . . .

Slater   Go on. You'll feel better. Let the tension out. (*Beat.*)

Kirk   The young lady with the long blonde hair. And the nice tits.

Slater   There. Feels better, doesn't it? Now you've said it, it's like you've held them in your hands . . . or had them in your mouth, all soft and wet. (*Beat.*) No, I wasn't speaking metaphorically.

Kirk   Is that why you came on your own?

Slater   I never come on my own.

Kirk   I'll rephrase that . . .

Slater   Don't bother. The reason that I came on my own is that I came on my own.

Kirk   I meant without your husband.

Slater   Oh, him.

Kirk   He was invited.

Slater   What, come as a couple and miss out on any action? Fuck off.

Kirk   I see.

Slater   Yeah, I'm primed. You got any drugs? (*Beat.*)

Kirk   I don't . . . use drugs.

Slater   Well it's a good job I dropped that tab of E when I came through security, then. (*He laughs.*) You think I'm joking?

Kirk   I don't know . . .

Slater   I asked the security guy for some water, said I felt faint, and popped a love pill.

Kirk   And how does it make you feel? (*Beat.*)

Slater   Warm and dirty. Like a little girl.

Kirk   You don't seem like a little girl to me.

Slater   Oh, I am, I'm just a ickle girlie. And you're just a naughty boy. (*She stands and refills their glasses.*) I saw you on *Newsnight* last week.

Kirk   Yes? Good, wasn't I?

Slater   Dunno. I had the sound off. But never wear beige is all I'm saying.

Kirk   I thought my suit conveyed a sense of light-humoured gravitas.

Slater   Nah. You came across like some ageing snake-oil salesman. (*Beat.*)

Kirk   Which is exactly what I am! (*He finds this very funny.*) No, I'm sorry. I bow to your superior knowledge in these things. The beige suit . . . (*He draws his finger across his throat.*)

Slater   How big is it?

Kirk   How big is what?

Slater   The amount of money you're going to offer me.
(*Beat.*)

Kirk   Substantial. But let's not get onto that straight away.

Slater   You want seduction before transaction, right?

Kirk   I just want to get to know you.

Slater   You don't have the time, bub. (*Beat.*)

Kirk   I can't believe we've never met before.

Slater   You should get out more.

Kirk   I suppose you're to be found in all the usual places.

Slater   Ooh, I hope not. But, yeah, I suppose I am.

Kirk   And I make it policy not to hang out where my
people might be. It's important to keep a distance, maintain
the mystique.

Slater   You 'hang out' do you?

Kirk   I believe that's the expression.

Slater   Another middle-aged man aching to be a trendy
young thing again.

Kirk   Again? No. I was never trendy. I was never really
young, come to that. (*Beat.*) Actually, there's a lot of bullshit
talked about youth. If somebody came in here now and
offered me my youth to live over again, or some serious
money, I'd go for the money. Every time.

Slater   I thought you'd already sort of done that.

Kirk   What, sold my soul? In a way. (*Beat.*) The same goes
for you. I'm going to offer you some very serious money to do
. . . what you do. No constraints, no demands. Just to do . . .
what you do. (*Beat.*)

Slater   Right. So let's talk about your penis. How big is
that? (*Beat.*)

Kirk   Substantial . . . enough.

Slater   Well, I don't know about that. Sounds to me like another way of saying average.

Kirk   Yes, average would do.

Slater   Well, tough. I read a feature in *Cosmo* that said that eighty per cent of men who described their schlongs as 'average' actually wished they were bigger. Do you wish your dick was bigger?

Kirk   No, I'm quite satisfied.

Slater   You might be satisfied, buster, but what about the girls?

Kirk   Well, I've never had any complaints.

Slater   Oh, yeah? Just because she doesn't grab hold of it and say: 'that is the most derisory apology for a cock I've ever been unfortunate enough to have in my hand' doesn't mean she's not thinking it. You should listen to girls talking some time.

Kirk   Really? I thought you'd have better things to talk about.

Slater   Oh, you know how it is . . . three in the morning, high as kites, the conversation turns to the deficiencies of male genitalia. Personally, the only cock I'm interested in probably doesn't exist. It's a great big thing. Definitely not 'average' or 'substantial enough'. I have in mind a living fucking salami. (*Beat.*)

Kirk   Tell me . . . were you, at all . . . abused, as a child? (*She laughs.*)

Slater (*beat*)   Is that what you think? That any woman who's upfront about sex was ipso facto an abused child?

Kirk   I read the papers, that's all.

Slater   Or maybe you're intimidated. (*Beat.*) Maybe that's why men abuse in the first place.

Kirk   You could be right. I believe the reason that men were excluded from childcare for centuries was so that they'd be out of harm's way, as it were. The upper classes, for instance, are so terrified of their own urges that they have little or nothing to do with the raising of their children. First a nanny, and then they ship them off to public school.

Slater   Where they all abuse each other in any case.

Kirk   No system's perfect. (*He smiles and holds his glass out. She refills it.*)

Slater   Do I get to see it, then? (*Beat.*)

Kirk   I fear you'd be disappointed.

Slater   So what's new? (*She sits with her legs apart and her feet splayed out.*) Come on. I'm sat here in my best fuck-me shoes. I think I deserve a glimpse of your mighty organ, don't you?

Kirk   You want me just to . . . take it out. . . ?

Slater   Isn't that what you do? Call a meeting, summon the guys, huddle in the office and slap them on the table?

Kirk   Now you *are* being metaphorical. (*Beat.*)

Slater   You don't really think I want a peek at your pecker, do you? (*Beat.*)

Kirk   The truth is, you're probably the only person I'd do it for. I don't know why.

Slater   Because you think it would turn me on.

Kirk   That would be my hope.

Slater   Which would turn *you* on.

Kirk   Or perhaps you'd . . . understand.

Slater   Oh, I understand. (*She takes out a cigarette.*) Light me.

Kirk   I don't smoke. (*She takes out her lighter and hands it to him. As he holds it to her cigarette she touches his hand.*)

Slater   Thanks. (*She takes the lighter back.*) It's a Dunhill. The lighter.

Kirk   What does that mean?

Slater   It means it's fucking expensive. Or vice versa. (*Beat.*) As Dorothy Parker would say.

Kirk   Yes, I recognise the quotation.

Slater   In case you think I'm dumb.

Kirk   Why would I think that?

Slater   Well, look at me. Skirt up round my arse and a mouth like a sewer.

Kirk   I see past all that.

Slater   And what do you see?

Kirk   What do you want me to see? (*Beat.*)

Slater   My knickers?

Kirk   Very nice.

Slater   La Perla. Silk. Fucking expensive.

Kirk   Or vice versa.

Slater   If I *must* have something riding up my crack, I'm going to make damn sure it's silk, thank you very much. How about you?

Kirk   Calvin Klein.

Slater   Nice touch. Your idea?

Kirk   Yes, why?

Slater   It doesn't feel like you, somehow. Not Calvin Klein.

Kirk   It's true. (*Beat.*) Is it that you're supposed to be cleverer than you look, and I'm supposed to be duller?

Slater   We don't dress to tell the truth about ourselves.

Kirk   Maybe not.

Slater   Come on then, show me how clever you are. Let's see your Calvins. (*He smiles.*) Come on. (*She gets up.*) Just the pants, nothing else. (*She goes to him, and as if handling something very delicate, undoes his trousers. She pulls his shirt to one side with her fingertips and takes a good look.*)

Kirk   Satisfied?

Slater   Never. (*She turns away and bends down for the champagne bottle. She fills their glasses, then bends down and puts the bottle and her glass on the floor. Still bending down, she does up his trousers again. She picks up her glass and stands with her back to him. He stares at her.*) What do you think of my arse?

Kirk   Very nice.

Slater   Come on. Let me hear some poetry, some filth. Come on.

Kirk   Do you think you really ought to have taken that pill?

Slater   I want you to unlock it all. Say the things you only ever think and never own up to. I do it all the time.

Kirk   That's what you're paid to do.

Slater   You're undressing me, aren't you? (*Beat.*) Mentally?

Kirk   Yes.

Slater   You're pulling my skirt up and running your fingers over the silk, feeling me firm and warm underneath, then pulling the knickers down to my knees and touching me ever so gently in the small of the back so that I lean forward, pulling the cheeks apart. And now you're kneeling with your face just an inch from me. I can feel your breath and you can smell me. Do I smell familiar or strange? And you're rubbing your face against me and I start to move my hips, side to side, backwards and forwards, and I'm opening up further as you start to use your tongue on me. And it's all moist and dark and warm and we're fusing into one another because we both want the same thing as we rock and pulse with the same rhythm, oh yeah, yeah. (*Beat.*) What *are* all these fucking trophies? (*Beat.* **Kirk** *is spellbound, staring at her, unable to speak. She turns round.*) I love pornography, don't you? Lucrative *and* fun.

Kirk   I prefer the real thing.

Slater   Oh, baby, it *is* the real thing.

Kirk   I always find it leaves me wanting more.

Slater   That's the point. That's why we get hooked on it. It's like a smart drug.

Kirk   But, like with any drug, I imagine, I want more. (*Beat. She goes and stands in front of him.*)

Slater   Go on.

Kirk   I feel self-conscious.

Slater   Have you got a hard on? (*Beat.*)

Kirk   Sort of.

Slater   What's it like? (*Beat.*) Would you like me to touch it?

Kirk   Yes.

Slater   How? (*Beat.*) Go on.

Kirk   I can't.

Slater   Yes you can. Do you want me to hold it? (*He nods.*) Gently? Or hard? (*He swallows.*)

Kirk   Hard.

Slater   And how does that feel? (*He breaks away.*)

Kirk   I'm sorry . . . I can't . . .

Slater   Maybe this isn't going to work out.

Kirk   No . . . yes . . . I mean . . .

Slater   There's something you want really bad, isn't there?

Kirk   Bad-ly. It's an adverb . . .

Slater   Isn't there?

Kirk   Yes.

Slater   What is it?

Kirk   I don't know. (*Beat.*)

Slater   You've got the money. You can have anything you want. (*Beat.*) But maybe that's it. Maybe it's nothing to do with money.

Kirk   Everything's something to do with money. (*Beat.*)

Slater   I don't think I could have sex if I was poor. I don't think I'd enjoy it very much. Fact, I think I'd kill myself if I was poor. Tie a silk scarf round my neck and hang myself from a tree with little apples growing in it.

Kirk   Why an apple tree?

Slater   Just something I remember.

Kirk   Nature.

Slater   Probably. (*She shudders.*) Ugh . . . poverty. Just the thought.

Kirk   Don't you find it stimulating? I do. It's important that when I walk out of the office there are beggars on the streets. It's important that when I'm being driven from one meeting to the next that I glimpse people with nothing. We need to be reminded of the depths, to look down occasionally into something terrible. And keep our balance. (*Beat.*) But it means . . . nothing can be ordinary. (*Beat.*) I often wonder what ordinary people *do*.

Slater   The poor saps do time. They do all the ordinary things, fill up their allotted span with crap. Like prisoners sewing mailbags, walking round the exercise yard, banged up in their little cells. (*Beat.*) You were ordinary once.

Kirk   So were you.

Slater   But we were given a get-out-of-jail-free card.

Kirk   Yes.

Slater   And now nothing will ever be ordinary again. (*Beat.*)

Kirk   I feel I'm getting to know you. (*Beat.*) Do you know what I'd like?

Slater   Tell me.

Kirk   I'd like to be at my desk and know that you were somewhere down the corridor. I'd like to pick up the phone and tell you what I was thinking, and for you to be thinking the same thing.

Slater   And what would we be thinking? (*Beat.*)

Kirk   Something unthinkable. It's all that's left. (*Beat.*)

Slater   I'd enjoy being somewhere down the corridor. You'd itch and I'd scratch.

Kirk   Mmm.

Slater   Would it be OK if I fucked people in my office?

Kirk   Why not? I have.

Slater   So *Private Eye* were telling the truth.

Kirk   For once. (*He laughs.*) Actually, they don't know the half of it.

Slater   Anybody I know?

Kirk   I shouldn't think so. (*Beat.*)

Slater   Are you lonely? (*Beat.*)

Kirk   Restless. (*Beat.*)

Slater   I sort of had the idea that you were cruel.

Kirk   Why?

Slater   Things you hear, things you read.

Kirk   Well don't believe anything the press says about me, it's all jealousy and spite.

Slater   Are you cruel in bed?

Kirk   I don't know. What *is* 'cruel in bed'?

Slater   Oh, you know . . . biting, gouging, scratching . . . hurting. Ropes, belts, chains, dildoes, bite-marks, bruises, blood. Asphyxiation, gags, blindfolds, fag-butts, blades, manacles, handcuffs, flames. (*Pause.*) Anything there up your street?

Kirk   Honestly?

Slater   What else? (*Beat.*)

Kirk   It all sounds . . . very promising.

Slater   Well it's not a set menu. You're supposed to use your imagination. (*Beat.*) Well?

Kirk   I've told you, I'm not very good at talking about it. (*Beat.*)

Slater   I have to hear it from your lips. Otherwise it's no-go, you know that, don't you? You've got to sink right down in it.

Kirk   Why?

Slater   So we know that that's where we are. Any other way and we would just be ordinary. You want to purchase the quality service I provide, and I want to deliver. But we have to have a union of interest first, so we both know we're transgressing. Face it, we're slaves to our culture and the only freedom we know is to be monstrous. Understand?

Kirk   Yes. I get it.

Slater   And? (*Beat.*)

Kirk   I'd like to tear you into pieces. I'd like to run my hands over your body and hook my fingers into the little cracks and crevices, everywhere you sweat . . . (*Beat.*)

Slater   Close your eyes. (*He does.*)

Kirk   And I want to take your hands and force them into you, and put them in your mouth, and I want to pull your legs wide apart until you scream –

Slater   I'm rubbing myself –

Kirk   And grab your breasts so hard there are bruises in the shape of my fingers –

Slater   I love that pain – (*She takes out a cigarette and lights it.*)

Kirk   And your face is covered, you could be anybody –

Slater   Just a body –

Kirk   I want to make new holes in you and fuck them –

Slater   Yeah –

Kirk   And pull your arms behind your back until they crack, and yank your head up by the hair and press my thumbs into your eyes while I come down your throat. (*Beat.*)

Slater   More.

Kirk   I can't.

Slater   I'm coming too.

Kirk   I want – (*He breaks away quickly, gasping. He stands, breathing hard, eyes still closed.*)

Slater   Well. Whoever would have imagined? (*He opens his eyes and smiles.*)

Kirk   You're extraordinary.

Slater (*she pours more champagne*)   See, all you need is permission. A presence that tells you to do whatever you want to do. And that's pornography.

Kirk   And is it a good thing?

Slater   Good, bad, what's the difference? Who can agree any more? People have been given permission and you can't revoke that without becoming very, very unpopular. (*Beat.*) As it happens, I don't recognise good and bad in *anything*. There's only what's allowed and what isn't. Every time I have an orgasm, another moral distinction goes out the window. (*There's a knock on the door.*)

Kirk   Come in. (*The door opens and* **Drummond** *comes in with a bottle of champagne. He too wears a morning suit.*)

Drummond   Refreshment?

Kirk   Good man. (**Drummond** *pops the cork.*)

Drummond   Are we celebrating?

Kirk   Ask Nikki.

Slater   I never *stop* celebrating.

Drummond   But have we, y'know, have we got a deal?
(**Kirk** *looks at* **Slater**.)

Slater   Let's see it on the table. (**Drummond** *laughs*.)

Drummond   I love that. She does that all the time.

Kirk   Really?

Drummond   Yeah, it creases me up.

Kirk   Good. OK, Nikki, I want you to have a whole page
in Features. And I want to make you Associate Features
Editor.

Slater   Features . . .

Drummond   Well, it's more lifestyle, really. The way we
live now.

Kirk   Zeitgeist.

Drummond   Exactly. We're kicking around the idea of
renaming the supplement just that: Zeitgeist.

Kirk   I want to break down the walls of stuffiness and
reverence. And your writing is a byword for iconoclasm . . .
look, what we call it doesn't really matter. What matters is
that we make it new. We need a new take on the world,
otherwise pretty soon we're going to start losing readers in
droves.

Slater   Don't you mean start losing even *more* readers in
droves?

Kirk   It's not that bad yet. Our core readership has held,
they always will. But they're –

Slater   Dying off –

Kirk   Not getting any younger.

Drummond   The intention, Nikki, is to stay right of centre
but not slavishly Tory-party-right-or-wrong right of centre.
No, the terrain we want to inhabit is the ex-Thatcherite keep
the reforms going till the job's done even if it's New Labour
that has to finish the job kind of terrain. (*Beat.*)

Kirk Most of all we want to put back into the paper intellectual vigour coupled with a sheer sense of fun.

Slater Ooh, sounds like a job for me.

Drummond Absolutely.

Slater But Features, well . . .

Drummond What?

Slater I think I'm ready for something a little more demanding.

Drummond Such as.

Slater I want to play on the grown-up pages, please.

Drummond Well, I don't know, I mean . . . (*He looks at* **Kirk**.)

Kirk I think that might be a wonderful idea. (*Beat.*)

Drummond Does this square with, uh. . . ?

Kirk Perfectly.

Drummond It'd mean . . .

Kirk Yes.

Drummond Fine.

Kirk Let's clean out the stables. Trim some fat. Hoover in the corners.

Slater I'll get my pinny on.

Kirk 'Nikki Slater. The Voice of Unreason.'

Drummond That's great.

Kirk I was joking.

Drummond Yeah, of course.

Kirk What would be your considered opinion of our non-news coverage, Nikki? (*She puts her fingers down her throat and gags.*) Is Snape waiting?

Drummond Yeah, he's out front.

Kirk Let's have him in.

Drummond   Right.

Kirk   And Drummond . . . more champagne.

Drummond   Right. (*He goes.*)

Slater   You've already got this worked out.

Kirk   More or less. You're my catalyst. How does that feel?

Slater   Exciting.

Kirk   Yes, it is, sort of. (*Beat.*)

Slater   You know Drummond's a wanker, don't you?

Kirk   I do. I inherited him.

Slater   So he's strategic . . .

Kirk   He's been a great help, he's good with the younger people. But I fear his prospects may not be too secure, long-term.

Slater   Good. (*Beat.*) I have one question. The Boss. What's he really like to work for?

Kirk   I have *carte blanche* for as long as I deliver, same deal as everyone. Same deal as you'll get.

Slater   And who decides if I'm failing to deliver?

Kirk   I call him, or he calls me, and *we* decide. (*Beat.*) He's very keen to meet you, by the way.

Slater   Do I have to suck his dick?

Kirk   He's a Christian.

Slater   So?

Kirk   So sucking his dick won't be necessary. (*Beat.*) People assume that he must be a terrible sleazeball, given some of the papers he owns, but he always says: 'I give the people what *they* want, not what *I* want.'

Slater   And happily, the two seem to coincide.

Kirk   That's his genius. He's a salesman, pure and simple.

Slater   Don't get me wrong, I think he's God. (*The door opens and* **Drummond** *comes in with* **Ray Snape**, *who is clearly a bit drunk. He sees* **Slater** *and stiffens.*)

Kirk   Snape.

Snape   What's this? A gang-bang? Sorry, sport, not with that old slapper.

Kirk   Do you two know each other?

Snape   No bloody fear. I know *of* her, I've seen her picture in the paper, seen her on the damn television. But *know* her? No bloody fear.

Slater   Who's this cripple?

Snape   Madam, I am perfectly fit and well, thank you.

Slater   Not for much longer.

Snape   Oh my God, I know you try to write like Norman Mailer on a bad day, but I didn't know you behaved like that too. (**Slater** *goes to him and knees him hard between the legs.* **Snape** *collapses in agony.*)

Slater   Who *is* this creep?

Kirk   Snape. Features.

Slater   Hang on, Raymond Snape?

Kirk   Yes.

Slater   Raymond Snape who reviewed my novel?

Kirk   Oh my God, he didn't, did he?

Slater   Too bloody right, he did. (*She kicks* **Snape**. *He screams.* **Kirk** *pulls her away as* **Drummond** *shields* **Snape**.) I've been dying to do that for nine months, you elitist bastard.

Kirk   Come on, leave him alone.

Slater   Do you know what he said about my book?

Kirk   I'm guessing here, but I suspect he didn't like it.

Slater   His exact words were: 'Do not read this book. It is spectacularly abysmal pornographic trash.'

Snape (*feebly*)   It was!

Slater   Yeah? So I don't see your point, buster. You think it's easy to write trash? It *was* exactly what it was *meant* to be. It wasn't another fucking Hampstead novelette or a book by one of your mates on the Nature Of Time. Jeez, all those fucking novels about 'What is the Nature Of Time?'. I'll tell you what the Nature Of Time is, sunshine, it's somewhere in the Nature of six o'clock and time for a drink.

Snape   She's mad! Malcolm, she's bloody raving, listen to her.

Slater   You and your highbrow con. What was that shit last week? About Derrida?

Snape   Oh, it was only an in-depth profile of possibly the world's most influential living philosopher.

Slater   Bollocks. It was a pile of crap written by some academic shithead who's never put a foot in the real world. People don't want that tat. They want to know what I, or someone like me, thinks about Derrida. They don't want to know about Derrida – who the fuck does? – they want to know about *us*. Because they're the *same* as us. Who in the world buys a paper in the morning hoping to discover nestling within its pages an in-depth profile of possibly the greatest philosopher in the world, Monsieur Jacques Fucking Derrida? Wise up, shitforbrains, you're pissing in the wind.

Snape   What is she raving about?!

Kirk   Why don't you have a seat?

Snape   Thanks. (*He sits, gingerly.*)

Drummond   Nikki, more champagne. (*He fills her glass.*)

Slater   How's your nuts, Raymond?

Snape   I'll sue you for assault. I have witnesses.

Kirk   We don't sue our colleagues, Snape.

Snape   Sorry? (*Beat.*) What?

Kirk   Nikki's joining the paper.

Snape   Oh, come on, look . . . (*He looks at* **Drummond**.) Rob. . . ?

Drummond   Bit of a coup, eh, Ray?

Snape   You can't, it's . . . I mean . . . what on earth is she going to do on *our* paper?

Kirk   What she always does. She's going to write a provocative and witty column. Oh, and she's joining the Features editorial team.

Snape   What? That's outrageous.

Slater   Outrageous! We'll have a page called that. Each week, a feature on something wild . . . cults, sex, fashion, pop, did I say sex. . . ?

Snape   This is a gag, Malcolm, tell me it's a gag.

Kirk   No gag.

Slater   And I'll be theatre critic. I've always wanted to close a show and put some luvvies on the dole.

Snape   We already have a theatre critic.

Slater   That's me. The wasp at the picnic. (*Beat.*) Then I'll move on to movies.

Snape   We already have a film critic.

Slater (*laughing*)   Film?!

Kirk   Some of those guys have become a little . . . predictable.

Snape   Yes, predictably good.

Slater   Oh my Gawd . . .

Snape   They have authority, our readers respect their judgement . . .

Slater   The only people who respect the critics' judgement are people who never go out and *see* anything.

Kirk   And we want to be a newspaper for people who go out.

Drummond   Profile-wise. (*Beat.*)

Snape   Are you all pissed? Has someone spiked the booze? (*Beat.*) If it's a joke, I'm not seeing the funny side. Plus, it would be quite nice to be able to leave the office behind for just one day in the year. Well?

Kirk   Snape, *we* are the office. If I call you in here to discuss the future development of the paper, then that is what you do. If you want to leave the office behind for half a second, you're no good to me. You are bought and paid for, every hour of every day. There's no clocking off. So, if I have an idea that I want to run past you, you come, and you listen. I don't care if you're eating, sleeping, shafting Her Majesty the Queen or having a bloody baby, you come. And you listen. (*Beat.*)

Snape   Sorry.

Kirk   Good.

Snape   So. (*Beat.*) Could I have some of that champagne? (**Drummond** *fills his glass.*) Thanks. OK, Malcolm, shoot.

Kirk   Shoot what?

Snape   Let's hear it.

Kirk   Am I penetrating anywhere near your brain's conscious level of activity? Do they teach you nothing at Cambridge? Jesus Christ, are you fucking deaf?

Snape   No, I'm just not sure . . . what you're proposing. (*Beat.*) Is she really . . . I mean. . . ?

Drummond   Malcolm, can I? (**Kirk** *nods.*) Ray, listen. A newspaper is a living thing, and all living things have to adapt themselves to changing circumstances.

Snape   Well, obviously . . .

Drummond   In our case, the most vital part of our existence is our relationship with our readers. They regard us as an old friend, and we bring them a sense of shared experience, a community of thought and ideas that binds us together in a seamless web.

Snape   Absolutely, one hundred per cent.

Drummond   But we have a problem with our readers, Ray, to wit: there are no longer enough of the fuckers. (*Beat.*) Now, Ray, you're the editor. What do you do?

Snape   Well . . .

Drummond   That was rhetorical, Ray. *I'll* tell you what you do. You attract new readers. There. You change the nature of the paper just enough to bring in the new punters, while reinforcing its core strengths.

Snape   But when Internews bought the paper, you gave all sorts of pledges that this wouldn't happen.

Drummond   Six months, that was how long we said it would take before we could give an accurate vision of the paper's future.

Kirk   And the six months is up. (*Beat.*)

Snape   So what *is* your vision of the paper's future? I mean, we can't make it any cheaper or we'll be giving it away.

Kirk   Cheaper is not a word I relish.

Snape   Well . . .

Kirk   Competitive is a much better word.

Snape   It means the same. (*Beat.*)

Kirk   I see some fresh thinking is needed. I take it, Snape, that you've not yet availed yourself of one of our motivational courses.

Snape   On the contrary, I have endured two days in whatever god-awful hotel it was, being talked down to in a Home Counties whine by a couple of mediocre sportsmen who had half-digested an American business efficiency

manual, and combined it with the psychology necessary to
motivate an especially dim under-fives rounders team. I
have spent two days of grinning humiliation, herded up,
ordered round, lectured, patronised. And the only thing I
learned was: if it isn't blindingly bloody obvious, if it
contains the merest hint of ambiguity, of human personality,
chuck it overboard. And if one is uncomfortable with this
simplistic potty training for the professional classes, or if,
heaven forbid, one is even mildly critical of it, then one is a
deviant, to be shunned by the group and bullied by the
leaders. When I arrived home, my wife asked me what it was
like, and all I could say was: it was like *Lord of the Flies*. (*Beat*.)

Kirk   The problem here is hostility. It's not just the courses
– which I must say most of our employees find extremely
rewarding – it's the whole culture to which you're hostile. So
put yourself in my place. There's nothing that's going to
convince you to become a team player, is there?

Snape   No. Not the way you mean it. Because we don't
arrive for work every day in order to churn out a mass-
produced lump of plastic. We don't depend on all pushing
the right buttons at the right moment. We use our training
and our intellect to present the world to people in a way that
they appreciate, and which even possibly expands their
horizons a little.

Kirk   How quaint. You're the sort of newspaperman who
thinks that if he gets a fan letter from some sad old cow in
Guildford, then he deserves the Pulitzer Prize.

Snape   I happen to believe that we stand for something.

Kirk   The only thing *I* stand for is the National Anthem.

Drummond   Hey, Ray, wake up and smell the Java is all
we're saying.

Snape   God will you shut up?! What's happened to you?
You were never a very *good* journalist, but at least you were
serious. Now, since his appointment, you come on like some
babbling junior prefect. It's as if you've been brainwashed.

Kirk It's amazing what a little promotion and corresponding rise in salary can do.

Snape Perhaps, but you have to *want* to lose your self-respect to go in as deep as he has.

Drummond Careful, Ray, or I might have to ask Nikki to give you another little slap.

Slater Any time.

Drummond OK, you've taken the gloves off, let's put a few home truths in the frame, shall we? You're crap, Ray. So long as the readership was an obedient, self-improving flock of sheep, there was a job for you. But now they're demanding something different and you just want to fob them off with the same old pony, I'm afraid.

Snape Who exactly *is* it who's demanding this change?

Drummond The bastards who've fucked off! The tens of thousands of people who no longer find it necessary or even diverting to buy the paper on a Sunday, shithead. God, you make me angry. What is it you think you're protecting? And who from?

Kirk Rome. And we're the Barbarians at the gates. (*He laughs.*)

Snape Yes, actually. (*Beat.*)

Slater God, I hate you.

Snape Well, there's a comfort, at least.

Slater Your days are gone, sunshine. It's time to make way for the future.

Snape When do we get to the part where you take out your little red books and scream at me?

Kirk Wrong cultural revolution.

Snape Really? Doesn't feel like it. (*Beat.*)

Kirk Anyway, think what a refreshing challenge it will be to work with Nikki and the young team we're putting together.

Snape   I don't think you really mean that.

Kirk   Why not?

Snape   Because I don't think you really mean *any*thing. Nothing at all. You're shinning your way up the Internews corporate structure. That's the only reality you care about, and it isn't reality at all.

Slater   Can I kick him again?

Kirk   No.

Snape   Do, and woman or not, I swear I'll punch you.

Slater   You haven't got the balls.

Snape   You see . . . *that* is what I can't stand. You all seem to think that I lack the moral fibre for your brave new world because I would have qualms about hitting a woman – hitting anybody, for heaven's sake. But you pride yourselves on being able to call up this juvenile nastiness at the drop of a hat. It's hard to believe we've gone so far backwards in so short a time.

Slater   Honey, you're facing the wrong way. (*Beat.*)

Snape   So, do you fire me now, or what?

Kirk   Fire you? I'm not firing you.

Snape   You're demoting me and placing me in an intolerable working situation.

Kirk   Hell, you still get paid. But if you find that intolerable . . .

Snape   So I'm supposed to resign.

Kirk   I guess any man with any pride would probably have to.

Snape   I'll be talking to the Union about the way you've done this.

Kirk   Hmm, there's frightening.

Drummond   Like, we are really pissing ourselves here, Ray. (*They laugh.* **Snape** *stands.*)

Snape   Well. I don't know what to say. After fourteen years . . .

Kirk   We're not about to give you a gold watch, man. Depart. (**Snape** *stands a moment then moves as if to go.* **Drummond** *goes to him and steers him the other way.*)

Drummond   Not that way, Ray. Security will walk you out the front.

Snape   God, you're low. Hang on, my wife −

Drummond   Yes, give Sally my best, won't you. They'll send someone round for her, don't worry. There'll be a coachload of you going back to town.

Snape   What the hell is going on?

Slater   Looks like you're being escorted from the premises.

Kirk   It's an old tradition.

Snape   But I was invited!

Kirk   That was in another lifetime.

Snape   And who says I've resigned?

Kirk   Well, I don't want to haggle. OK, you're fired.

Snape   Like hell. I resign.

Kirk   Thank you. Now piss off.

Slater   Hey, if you ever write a book, I can guarantee you at least *one* review. (**Snape** *looks at her then goes*.) Ooh, I think I could use a Kleenex. I've gone all moist. (**Drummond** *gives her a lascivious look*.) Drummond, who's the gorgeous girl you were chatting up earlier? With the long blonde hair?

Drummond   Chatting up? Me?

Slater   Well, more sort of tripping over your tongue, really.

Drummond   Oh, you mean Natasha.

Slater   Mmm.

Drummond   She does occasional travel pieces for the magazine. I know she looks like a gold-plated bimbo, but she's actually got a couple of degrees.

Slater   Good. I want her.

Drummond   What, on Features?

Slater   That too. (*Beat.*)

Kirk   Seriously?

Slater   Yes. I want her to work with me. I want her to be my friend.

Drummond   Join the club.

Slater   I *am* the club. (*Beat.*) Can I have her?

Kirk   Is she good enough?

Drummond   Oh God, she'd walk into a job any day. But I think she likes her freedom.

Slater   Then dangle a big one in front of her.

Drummond   Malcolm? (*Beat.*)

Kirk   Offer her grade two.

Drummond   Grade two?! (**Kirk** *smiles and nods.*) OK.

Kirk (*looking at his watch*)   Well. I've got several people to sack before dinner. Better get on.

Slater   Yeah, chop chop.

Kirk   Let's discuss money later. Over dinner. You're on the big table with us.

Slater   Fine. And no cock-sucking.

Kirk   Only if you get desperate.

Slater   No fear. (*Beat.*) Hey . . . Zeitgeist. Spirit of the times. I dunno. What about Anschluss? (*Beat.*)

Kirk   Let's have a meeting to discuss it.

Slater   Great. I'll bring a salami. Later, boys. (*She goes.*)

Drummond   I couldn't half give her one.

Kirk   I don't think she really likes sex very much.

Drummond   You what?

Kirk   It's her currency, that's all. (*Beat.*)

Drummond   That's a bit fucking deep. (*He fills their glasses.*)

Kirk   The word is harlot.

Drummond   Ace writer, though.

Kirk   Oh, yes. Even if she doesn't know what an adverb is. Cheers. (*They drink.*)

Fade.

Section Two

The stage is split between a room in the house and the patio outside the window. The curtains in the room are closed. There is a table and chairs on the patio. Inside the room, with his back to us, stands **Viggers**, *dressed in a morning suit, his trousers round his ankles. He is having sex with a woman on her back on the table, unseen, except for her legs which are up around* **Viggers***'s waist. Her tights are still on her left foot, and dangle with her knickers from her ankle. They screw all the way through the scene,* **Viggers** *emitting the odd grunt or moan, the woman silent. At another small table sit* **Budge** *and* **Whistler**. **Whistler** *is dolefully munching his way through a plate of sandwiches and swigging champagne, while* **Budge** *is chopping cocaine on a mirror. They barely seem to notice* **Viggers***.*

Budge Thing about a morning suit, right, it carries a sense of dignity. It's a statement, right? It says: I've arrived, and it's important you know that. I accept the rules, I embrace the standards. The suit is a classic. Not flash, not tacky. I know the difference. Classic. Says it all, that. (**Whistler** *belches. Outside, from the bushes,* **Bob Coleman** *emerges, doing up his flies. As* **Budge** *continues talking,* **Coleman** *goes to the table and peers inside an empty champagne bottle. He walks a little way off.*) Same as the hair. You want the classic short back and sides. Public school, Guards, City short back and sides. With a nice dollop of old-fashioned glop on it. What I call a Cecil. (*Beat.*) As in: Parkinson.

Whistler Ah, the good Lord. (*He belches. Outside,* **Coleman** *is calling out to somebody.*)

Coleman I say! You! (*Beat.*) Yes! (*He motions to them to come to him and sits at the table.*)

Budge Yeah, see, he had it, the look. Totally convincing. And he had the voice, too. And what was his dad? Only a fucking train driver, right?! Total democracy. I mean, anyone can look like they own a business, run a health trust, edit a newsrag, run the country, you name it. You see them everywhere and they can't *all* be powerful. It's brilliant.

Whistler   Brilliant bollocks.

Budge   But look at the pride on those guys' faces. That's the payoff. (**Viggers** *groans*.) Go on, fill yer boots, my son. (*Outside, a* **Waiter** *arrives*.)

Coleman   Clear this away, would you? And bring another bottle. (*The* **Waiter** *looks peeved and goes*.)

Whistler   Parkinson looked like what he was. To wit: an oleaginous fraud.

Budge   Holy what?

Whistler   Oleaginous: oily or greasy.

Budge   Oh.

Whistler   Anyway, Parkinson went *au naturel*, didn't he? Threw away the grease and opted for a caring blowwave at the start of the nineties, this kinder, gentler decade in which we languish still.

Budge   You're missing the point about his hair. It's an old preparation. It's meant to look greasy.

Whistler   I'm not really talking about his hair . . .

Budge   What he had, right, was gravitas. (**Whistler** *splutters*.) See? That's why the point's gone straight past you. You don't read the signals because you come at it with the wrong attitude.

Whistler   And that's why you're paid twice as much as me to write half as much as me.

Budge   It's the fact that I know he's not a real toff that's the clincher, right? Because he knows I know. So we're both in there believing he is when we know he isn't.

Whistler   And what about me?

Budge   You're the bloke watching the magician who shouts out: I know how he does that. Which makes you very unpopular with the punters because we all know how it's done. We just pretend we don't.

Whistler   But why, for Christ's sake?

Budge   For a quiet life. People don't look at politicians any more and say: who's this lying, oleaginous bastard?

Whistler   *I* do.

Budge   Yeah, you and Jeremy Paxman. But *you* ain't people. People look at him and go: oooh, nice hair, nice suit. He looks like he might be able to run the country. Right? (**Viggers** *takes a breather and looks up.*)

Viggers   Budge. Fag. (**Budge** *gets up and takes a cigarette to* **Viggers** *and lights it for him as, outside, the* **Waiter** *arrives with a bottle of champagne and puts it on the table.*)

Coleman   What about glasses?

Waiter   There. (*He points at the glasses on the table.*)

Coleman   They're nothing to do with me.

Waiter   I'm supposed to be on my break.

Coleman   Heaven's sake, man, you're a waiter. Go and wait. (*The* **Waiter** *raises his eyebrows and goes.*)

Budge (*sitting and chopping again*)   But don't make the mistake of thinking that people don't know, because they *do* know. They're not stupid. They're saying: it's OK, we don't mind because you're doing exactly what we'd do. Which is, in my opinion, what democracy is all about.

Whistler   Doesn't it just tend to show how little imagination most people have?

Budge   Like I said, anything for a quiet life. Long as they're not putting people in death camps and the superstores are stocked, who's complaining? The trick is not to take it too serious.

Whistler   I need a piss. (*He gets up and goes as, outside,* **Coleman** *has taken out his Dictaphone and speaks into it.*)

Coleman   Paragraph: Whilst taking a breather from the festivities at the wedding of the year, I happened to come across a spotty youth masquerading as a waiter. When I attempted to avail myself of his services, he told me, with a barely concealed snarl: 'You'll have to wait, I'm on my tea-break.' Well, you'll have to excuse me, but a waiter at a function taking time off for a tea-break? Isn't that rather like a restaurant closing for lunch? (*Beat.*) Somewhere, presumably, General Secretary Bert Plonk of UWAT, the union of waiters and allied trades, has decreed that all operatives shall be given a statutory break, during which the provision of food and drink will be temporarily suspended. I ask you, what poppycock! (*He switches off the machine as the* **Waiter** *arrives with some glasses.*) How long is your 'break'?

Waiter   Fifteen minutes.

Coleman   Fine, well take it now, and I shall expect you back here with another bottle in twenty minutes. (*Beat. The* **Waiter** *shrugs and starts to go as* **Percy Wadsworth** *arrives, smiling, and sits. The* **Waiter** *goes. Inside,* **Budge** *is snorting a line of coke and offering some to* **Viggers**. *When he's done this, he starts chopping some more.*)

Wadsworth   Not speaking, Bob? (*Beat.*)

Coleman   Traitor. (*Beat.*)

Wadsworth   I take it you read my piece in the *Spectator*.

Coleman   Absolute bollocks. Wouldn't use it to wipe my arse.

Wadsworth   Can't we be civilised about it?

Coleman   No. (*Beat.*)

Wadsworth   Why did you run off like that? (*Pause.*) Bob, really . . .

Coleman   You make me very angry. (*Beat.*)

Wadsworth   Well, I apologise for that.

Coleman   I don't need your apologies. Save those for Margaret.

Wadsworth   Are we not allowed to change our minds?

Coleman   You don't change faith this late in the game.

Wadsworth   Bob, I'm aware that many strange things happened in the 1980s, but I didn't realise I had taken holy orders.

Coleman   We had a mission to change this country.

Wadsworth   Yes. And *didn't* we do well?

Coleman   We did *bloody* well.

Wadsworth   By chucking everybody in the deep end and seeing who swam and who sank. And now, seventeen years later, lying at the bottom of our pool is a sediment of sunken bodies. (*Beat.*)

Coleman   You've lost your bloody marbles. (**Wadsworth** *smiles.*) You don't just suddenly dump everything you've ever believed in. That's just childish. (*Beat.*)

Wadsworth   I'm afraid we're all as guilty as hell.

Coleman   Completely bonkers.

Wadsworth   'Where there is discord, may we bring harmony. Where there is darkness, may we bring light.' (*Beat.*) The words of a saint become the most cynical soundbite of all time. We began our rule by spitting in God's face. (**Coleman** *laughs.*)

Coleman   I deal with people, not with God.

Wadsworth   Not forever. (*Beat.*)

Coleman   Admit it, Percy, you drank yourself to a nervous breakdown. You lost the plot. And now everybody just wishes you'd bugger quietly off.

Wadsworth   And now that our culture no longer has room for intelligence or conscience, I shall. (*Inside,* **Whistler** *has come back in. He watches* **Budge** *chopping the coke.*)

Whistler   How long d'you have to do that for?

Budge   Long as you like. I happen to find it very
therapeutic.

Whistler   Funny habit.

Budge   It's not a habit, it's a recreation.

Whistler   It looks like a habit.

Budge   I don't do it habitually, I do it occasionally, for
recreation.

Whistler   When *I* see you, you're always doing it.

Budge   When *you* see me, yeah, because I'm always
relaxing when you see me.

Whistler   Well then, either you're always relaxing, or
that's a habit.

Budge   I try to live a stress-free life.

Whistler   And does it work?

Budge   Dunno. I'm always too coked up to notice.
(**Viggers** *groans and pauses*. **Budge** *looks up*. **Viggers** *resumes*.)
No. I thought he'd finished for a minute. Are you having a
go?

Whistler   No, mate, not for me. Sloppy seconds, ugh.

Budge   He's wearing a raincoat.

Whistler   Yeah, I know, but all the same . . .

Budge   I heard you were more into, you know, watching
it . . .

Whistler   Pardon?

Budge   I was told you were keener on the cinematic
potential of intimate human contact.

Whistler   Who by?

Budge   A little bird.

Whistler   What have you been told?

Budge   It's no big deal. Only that you were the bloke to ask if I was ever in the market for mucky vids. Dave Whistler, Sportsdesk. I wrote it down.

Whistler   Look, Budge, I can only think of one person who could have told you that.

Budge   Drummond, yeah. (*He begins rolling a twenty-pound note.*)

Whistler   Drummond speaks to you?

Budge   Yeah.

Whistler   He speaks to you?

Budge   Where d'you think he gets his coke? (*Beat.*) No, I'm only joking. (*He snorts his line and hands the note to* **Whistler**.)

Coleman   I happen to know that some of the things you've written have hurt Margaret very deeply.

Wadsworth   You flatter me. (**Whistler** *has snorted his line.* **Budge** *takes the mirror and the note over to* **Viggers**, *who breaks off long enough to snort his line.*)

Coleman   Most people write it off as the vicious vendetta of a bitter old soak.

Wadsworth   Most people?

Budge (*sitting again*)   I had lunch with Drummond last week, as a matter of fact.

Whistler   Lunch? You had lunch with the Deputy Editor?

Budge   Well, liquid lunch. In a lap-dancing club. I think it was his way of saying he likes me.

Whistler   Likes you?

Budge   Yeah. Admires my journalistic abilities.

Whistler   I'm trying to comprehend this. Drummond took *you* to lunch?

Budge   Yeah. I reckon he was, like, sounding me out.

Whistler   For what?

Budge   Some kind of move.

Whistler   What did he say? I mean, actually *say*?

Budge   Fuck that, I was on the Bacardis, how should *I* know. (**Coleman** *stands and looks at the view.*)

Whistler   I don't believe a word of this. *They* just do not socialise with *us*.

Budge   He wasn't socialising with us, he was socialising with me.

Wadsworth   Lovely view.

Coleman   Culpability Brown. Terrible vandal.

Budge   Talking of which, is it true about the videos?

Whistler   Yes.

Budge   You get all the continental stations?

Whistler   It's very simple.

Budge   Scramblers and all that malarkey, yeah?

Whistler   Yes.

Budge   And how many films have you got?

Whistler   About two hundred and fifty.

Budge   Get outta here.

Whistler   Why?

Budge   You're a fanatic.

Whistler   No, I'm a connoisseur.

Budge   D'you live on your own?

Whistler   That's right.

Budge   Well in that case, you're a sad, lonely wanker, mate. (*Beat.*) No, I'm only joking. (*Beat.*)

Wadsworth   My diaries are being edited for publication next year. (**Coleman** *shoots him a fierce glance.*)

Budge   Hard core, are they?

Whistler   Mostly.

Budge   *Very* hard core?

Whistler   Mostly.

Budge   Are they legal?

Whistler   Mostly not.

Budge   Can you chuck a couple my way?

Whistler   I'm not a sodding lending library.

Budge   I'll tell you what Drummond said.

Whistler   OK. But I want them back. And it's a tenner each. (*Beat.*) So, what's sir's preference?

Budge   Eh?

Whistler   Well . . . lesbian, groups, anal, animals, pissing. . . ?

Budge   I'm easy, mate.

Whistler   I'll throw in the new Buttman. Buttman goes to Rio.

Budge   And what does he do when he gets to Rio?

Whistler   He goes out on the streets with a camera and asks women if they'll fuck him. Personally, I think they're actresses, but opinions differ. And if they say yes, he takes them back to his hotel and fucks them up the backside for an hour.

Budge   A gentleman could do no less.

Whistler   Precisely.

Budge   Buttman, yeah. That sounds right up my alley.

Wadsworth   Is she here yet? Margaret?

Coleman   I couldn't tell you.

Wadsworth   Apparently, she's arriving by helicopter. The broomstick must be in for a service.

Budge   Buttman . . . (*He laughs.*)

Wadsworth   The thing is, Bob, I'm going to be dead quite soon. (*Beat.*) I am currently preoccupied with the process of making my peace with my God. (*Beat.*)

Coleman   I'm sorry. But it's no excuse.

Budge   D'you know how much this is all costing?

Whistler   Her or the coke?

Budge   Coke's a tenner a line. (*He grins.*) No, I mean the wedding.

Whistler   Dunno. Hundred thou?

Budge   What? Bollocks. Double it, mate, then add some.

Coleman   I don't know what to say.

Budge   That's the lot. Everything from start to finish. There's flying in celebs from all over the world for starters, then there's hiring the house and grounds, catering, marquees, fireworks, orchestra, fleet of executive buses to ferry all of us here from London . . .

Whistler   It's obscene.

Budge   Imagine writing the cheque, yeah? Quarter of a million.

Whistler   Obscene . . .

Budge   No, Dave, excuse me mate, but fucking strange women up the backside in front of a camera is obscene. Coughing up a wedge for your only daughter's wedding is an act of paternal affection.

Whistler   My arse. It's business. We gobble up the groom's US cable operation, he gets a seat on the Internews board and a lifetime shagging the boss's daughter.

Budge   So it's not *all* wine and roses . . .

Whistler   Quite. Take a look at the bride. We are not talking love match here. No, what these guys are doing is carving out a parallel power zone. Real power in this day and age lies in information and communication, and whoever owns the hardware has the power. So, we get colonies and empires and rise and fall, only it's happening in a parallel world. But because the media decides so much of what is seen to happen in the real world, they're controlling its destiny. And there it is: the world is run by a power which has few rules and no history. (*Beat.*) This coke's good, isn't it?

Budge   You just enjoy it, mate.

Coleman   It *is* a lovely view. I'll allow you that. (*He pours them more champagne.*)

Whistler   So, are you going to tell me how you and Drummond come to be eyeing up the totty all cosy together of a lunchtime?

Budge   It was just casual.

Whistler   Or maybe it was business. (*He looks at the coke.*)

Budge   Oh, come on, that was a joke. As if I'd really be dealing coke to the Deputy Editor.

Coleman   Could I ask you, Percy, as a former friend, to think very carefully before publishing?

Wadsworth   You're a journalist now, Bob. Don't you want to see the truth in print?

Coleman   Diaries are not the truth.

Whistler   He borrows my movies, but he doesn't like me, you know.

Budge   Who says?

Whistler   *He* does.

Budge   What? He said: Whistler, I don't like you?

Whistler   Funnily enough, that is exactly what he said.

Budge   No, bollocks.

Whistler   He said: Whistler, I don't like you. And he sent me on a course.

Budge   What, Beldon Hall?

Whistler   That's the one.

Budge   It's brilliant, that course.

Whistler   The rest of them were gung-ho like you. Except for Ray Snape from Features.

Budge   The Nerd.

Whistler   Yeah, that's him.

Budge   That's what Drummond calls him. The Nerd.

Whistler   Oh. So who else did you talk about at this lunch?

Budge   I dunno, I was leggo. (**Coleman** *walks towards the bushes.*)

Coleman   I just need to . . . uh . . .

Wadsworth   Prostate?

Coleman   You remembered. (*He goes into the bushes. Through the next section until* **Coleman** *returns,* **Wadsworth** *goes through a process which sees him begin to cry, softly at first, then full-on, then he stops, wipes his eyes and the twinkle returns.*)

Budge   What I want to know is why did he tell you he doesn't like you? I mean you must have done something naughty to upset him.

Whistler   Oh yeah. Didn't you read my end-of-season football round-up last year?

Budge   I expect so.

Whistler   Crap, wasn't it?

Budge   Dunno, mate.

Whistler   Well, it was. And why? Because my *real* end of season round-up was spiked. The reason being that it was less than fulsome in its praise of Satellite TV's effect on our national game. To wit: it's completely fucked it. So, Drummond called me in and explained ever so rudely that perhaps it wasn't the smartest career move ever to slag off the jewel in our company's broadcasting crown.

Budge   You can see his point.

Whistler   Most certainly. His point is: you are no longer free to write whatever you want. Your version of events must always take into account any business interest that Internews might have in your subject. You will not write anything harmful to our overall business strategy. You will obey orders.

Budge   Well, surely you're not going to slag off the company, are you? I mean, point one, they pay your wages.

Whistler   Only for the last six months. We were taken over, remember?

Budge   Not me, mate, I came with them. I don't see your problem, anyway. I reckon our Satellite football's top.

Whistler   Are you a football fan, Budge?

Budge   'Course.

Whistler   Yeah, who isn't these days? So who do you support?

Budge   United. (*Beat.*)

Whistler   Sutton? Cambridge?

Budge   There's only one United.

Whistler   No, actually there's quite a few.

Budge   And number one: Man United.

Whistler   Why the affection for a team from the other end of the country?

Budge   Top club, aren't they? Glamour, stars, heritage, they got the lot.

Whistler   And how often do you see them?

Budge   Never miss a match.

Whistler   In the flesh?

Budge   Bollocks. On the box. Hardly going to schlep all the way to fucking Manchester just for a football match, am I?

Whistler   Have you *ever* seen them play?

Budge   I get it. Trick question. Cups of Bovril and meat pies. Flat caps and rattles. Knowledgeable and witty working-class banter amid the camaraderie of the terraces. Entrance fee, match programme, pint after the game, five Woodbines and change from ten bob.

Whistler   You've never actually seen them play?

Budge   Not in the flesh. No.

Whistler   Have you ever been to a match at an Association Football-ground?

Budge   Hah! Yeah, last season. I was invited to Sugar's box at Spurs.

Whistler   And who were they playing?

Budge   Uh . . . Liverpool, no . . . the other one . . . Leeds. That's it, Leeds. I think.

Whistler   Who won?

Budge   Spurs. I think.

Whistler   Score?

Budge   Yeah, I did, as a matter of fact, after the game. (*Beat.*) There was a couple of goals. Least, I think that's what it means when the morons all jump up and down at the same time.

Whistler   Two one. Sheringham got the winner in the eighty-sixth minute. Bit of a fluke. Off the post and the back of a defender's head.

Budge   Whoah. Anorak city.

Whistler   Hardly. I was there reporting it.

Budge   And I was there being wined and dined, picking up some useful info. So we were both working.

Whistler   But I was there to watch the football. I actually had a tenuous connection to the twenty-two blokes running round the pitch.

Budge   And *I* got to talk to Alan Sugar. (*Beat.*)

Whistler   So. That's your only visit to a football ground.

Budge   Yeah.

Whistler   But you still feel qualified to take the piss when someone who lives for football says that we've lost something from the game. Bovril and flat caps, ho ho ho.

Budge   I just hate the fucking nostalgia. I live in the present. I want *now*. I don't want to be constantly lectured about how now isn't a patch on then.

Whistler   But what if it isn't?

Budge   I don't wanna know! (*Beat.*)

Whistler   You see, it's just that I remember when football teams weren't consumer items on a shelf. You didn't shop around and pick the team with the highest profile, image-wise. Your team chose you.

Budge   Yeah. All well and good when we lived in a small world, but hey, we're free to choose from wherever we want now. Now, we have mobility of the imagination.

Whistler   No, we have loss of identity.

Budge   It's only football!

Whistler   And there you have it. It's only football. Just another deep-rooted part of some people's lives past its sell-by date. Just something else to tart up and make some money out of.

Budge   Precisely. (**Coleman** *comes on from the bushes, doing up his flies. He pours champagne, then looks at his watch.*)

Wadsworth   She'll be here, Bob, don't worry.

Whistler   Are you, uh . . . if he ever finishes? (*He points to* **Viggers**.)

Budge (*quiet*)   No chance. You seen the needle marks on its arms? (*He mimes injecting himself.*)

Whistler   Oh my God . . .

Budge   I'm keeping it in my pants, cheers.

Whistler   Does Viggers know?

Budge   Wouldn't stop him if he did. He'd shag the crack of dawn if it had hairs on it. Olympic class, he is.

Whistler   Lucky, lucky man.

Coleman   I don't believe it! Some oafs are paddling in the lake.

Wadsworth   That'll be the tabloids. (*They laugh.*)

Budge   I take it you don't get a lot, Dave.

Whistler   *Any*. Don't get any.

Budge   Well, no offence, but maybe if you weren't sat at home all the time watching Scandinavians at it, you might actually get out and meet some real live women, y'know?

Whistler   Waste of time. The ones who'll talk to me don't shag, and the ones who shag won't talk to me.

Budge   But you must have . . . I mean, there must be someone who's talked to you *and* shagged.

Whistler   Oh yes. Maureen. We actually lived together for six months. She was very adventurous, if not especially attractive. Bit on the skinny side, really. And very unpredictable. She swallowed a bottle of sleeping pills one day.

Budge   Blimey, you *must* be crap, mate.

Whistler   Yeah, that's what *I* thought. So I moved out.

Budge   And what about Maureen?

Whistler   Oh, she died.

Wadsworth   We were very largely wrong, Bob.

Coleman   Cock.

Whistler   And now, my sex life, like your football life, is wholly voyeuristic.

Budge   I don't think I'd really put the two on a par myself.

Whistler   Maybe not. But sex, for me, is something other people do somewhere else, in a different time. And, odd as it may seem, they do it for *my* pleasure. But at least I know that what they do is only a parody of real sex. Pornography is pantomime sex, really. And all over the world, increasing numbers of people are growing up believing that what they see is what people really do. Or worse, what people really *should* do.

Budge   They know it's just a bit of fun.

Whistler   Do they really?

Budge   'Course they do.

Whistler   You've got a lot of faith in people.

Budge   I try not to act as if I know what's best for them, if that's what you mean.

Whistler   No, I mean, your idea of people is that they're all supersmart to the ways of the media. In your world we're all critics.

Budge   Because we've all been taught to read and write and operate the technology. The idea of education used to be that we were all capable of creating something, something original. Well . . . total bollocks, yeah? Instead, what you end up with is a nation of critics. We all know how it works.

Whistler   But knowing how it works doesn't mean you understand it.

Budge   Understanding's irrelevant. What counts today is that the audience controls the relationship. If they're bored, or confused, they fuck off, and *you* lose. In the old days they didn't dare. It was all so reverent and fucking polite. Now, it's in your face. It's democratic.

Whistler   I'm coming to like your idea of democracy less and less.

Budge   Because you're old-style, mate. You know your place, that's the trouble.

Whistler   Wait a minute . . . I'm supposed to be a radical consumer but a conformist worker.

Budge   Nice one.

Whistler   That's what you're saying.

Budge   Yeah. Kick up where you might have some effect.

Whistler   It must be the drugs. (*Beat.*) I'm going to ask for a new byline: Dave Whistler, Football Critic.

Budge   Yeah, look good on your CV.

Whistler   Why? Am I going somewhere?

Budge   Nah, you know what I mean.

Whistler   Only, I've been hearing a lot about CVs recently. Quite a few people have been writing them from what I hear.

Budge   Yeah? Well, it's a big company, isn't it? There's bound to be a lot of coming and going.

Whistler   The rumour mill says we're going downmarket. We're going to disappear even further into the middlebrow hinterland of middle England, apparently.

Budge   Sounds good, whatever it is.

Wadsworth   I'm going to call the diaries *Mea Culpa*. (*He and* **Coleman** *laugh.*)

Budge   And what if we were? What would you do? Hypothetically. Say I'm your new boss, or might be, depending on the outcome of this interview.

Whistler   Terrifying thought. (*He laughs.*)

Budge   Yeah. Innit?

Coleman   You're jumping ship at the wrong time, you know.

Budge   Would you stay on?

Wadsworth   I'm exercising my conscience.

Whistler   Yeah, I guess so.

Budge   That's cool, Dave, because I think you've got
something to offer the new-look paper, and I'd like to help
you discover just what it is. Now, say for the sake of argument
that me and Mike have been appointed to edit a whole new
section of the paper, right? A sort of pop and football fanzine
inside the Style Section. (*Beat.*) Like the sound of it?
Football, comedy, rock 'n' roll, it'll all be in there. You can
put Ruud Gullit, Oasis and Frank Skinner in the same
article.

Whistler   Why would you want to?

Budge   Because they're all within the frame of reference of
the sort of people we want to read *Whoosh!*.

Whistler   *Whoosh?*

Budge   *Whoosh* exclamation mark. That's just a dummy
title. It's meant to remind the lads of *Shoot*, the football
magazine.

Whistler   *Whoosh.*

Budge   Yeah, well, it's not set in concrete, y'know . . .

Whistler   I should hope not.

Budge   It's meant to be light-hearted, a bit of fun.
Scurrilous, sharp, a bit naughty −

Whistler   In a word: tabloid.

Budge   If you like.

Whistler   And how is this going to help me fulfil my hidden
potential?

Budge   *Fantasy Football*, right?

Whistler   What, on the telly?

Budge   Yeah. You got Frank and Dave, right, and all these
celebs and off-the-wall merchants, but you've also got . . .
what?

Whistler   A sofa? (*Beat.*) Beer? (*The penny drops.*) Stato.

Budge   Correct. The man with the knowledge. You've got the voice of authority stood there in pyjamas and a dressing-gown.

Whistler   So the only way we can be comfortable with knowledge is to dress it in something silly and take the piss.

Budge   Yeah, he's a trainspotter, but we need him, right? It reassures the unconvinced and the anoraks that deep down we're serious about this stuff. They have to believe that *we* believe it's important, otherwise they're turned off. (*Beat.*) The idea is, you have a column where you sound off, a bit tongue-in-cheek, y'know, send it all up a bit. But you get to say all the stuff you have to leave out now, about managers, directors, bungs, drugs, you know. And here, listen, we call it 'Whistler In The Dark'. (*Beat.*) Yeah?

Wadsworth   Thing is, Bob, you can't go out and create a wasteland and then pretend it's blooming with orchids.

Budge   Obviously, Satellite coverage, any deals involving the company, that's a no-go area, right?

Whistler   Ah. The catch.

Budge   Bottom line is, Dave, that Internews is going to do what it does, regardless. There's nothing you can do. Basically, it's onwards and upwards with the company, or get that CV printed. (*Beat.*) Fit in . . . or fuck off. (*Beat.*) How about it?

Whistler   Hypothetically?

Budge   Sure.

Whistler   You dream about this, don't you? Where you get to tell the boss what you think of him. The good guy storms the boardroom, and with one speech, he rights all the wrongs. After years banged up for a crime you didn't commit, you get the big courtroom scene where the truth is revealed and the bad guys are led off to the slammer. And the world carries on as it was meant to.

Budge   The trouble with fantasies, Dave, is they're a sign of impotence.

Whistler   Yeah, in truth, I'm not even allowed the dignity of a quiet grumble. And on top of that, I'm supposed to believe in the product as well.

Whistler   I don't want to lose my job. I love what I do. Up to a point, the point where I feel a hand on my shoulder, and a quiet voice saying 'that's enough, stop there'. Then I hate it. And I hate myself.

Wadsworth   Is that a helicopter?

Coleman (*excited*)   Where?

Wadsworth   Over there. (*He points up.* **Coleman** *looks.*)

Budge   Is that what you're going to tell Kirk and Drummond when they see you later on?

Whistler   How did you know about that?

Budge   If they asked you what I asked you . . .

Whistler   Is this serious?

Budge   You need to be straight in your own mind. You need to know what's on the table.

Whistler   Are you really being serious? (*Beat.*)

Coleman   I do believe it's her.

Budge   Yes.

Whistler   You sod. Why couldn't you just come out with it?

Budge   I need to know if I like you.

Whistler   And do you?

Budge   Let's just say if you were female, mate, I'd have it halfway down your throat.

Coleman   Oh my word, look, isn't it splendid?

Whistler   But Drummond doesn't like me.

Budge   If *I* like you, *he* likes you. Providing you stay within the brief.

Whistler   Remember the cage has bars.

Budge   Wicked. (*The* **Waiter** *appears with a bottle of champagne*.)

Coleman   No time for that now. She's here.

Wadsworth   Oh joy.

Coleman   Coming Percy? Or are you frit?

Whistler   Well, life's a prison, what the hell? (*He shakes hands with* **Budge**.)

Wadsworth   Lead on, Sir Bob, lead on. (*They go*.)

Budge   Let's find something to drink. Besides, he'll never finish while he can hear work going on. (*They stand and go to the door*.) See you in the champagne bar, Mick. (**Viggers** *grunts*.) Have one for me. (**Budge** *and* **Whistler** *go*. **Viggers** *climaxes. After all of a few seconds' reflection he pulls the condom off and drops it on the floor and pulls up his trousers. The* **Waitress** *sits up, blank*.)

Viggers   How much did we say? (*He's searching for his wallet*.)

Waitress   Thirty.

Viggers   Right . . . I don't suppose you take credit cards . . . (*He spots the rolled note on the mirror*.) Oh, hang on, you're in luck. (*He unrolls it and drops it on the table*.) Twenty all right? (*He goes. Outside, the* **Waiter** *takes out a cigarette and lights it. Inside, the* **Waitress** *sits on the table, staring ahead*.)

Fade.

Section Three

A small conservatory to the side of the house. **Toop** *and* **Brennan** *are sitting at a table. Sitting to one side, bored and forlorn, looking out at the grounds, is* **Alison Toop**.

Toop   OK. 'I have slept in the same bed as male friends many times, but any suggestion of homosexuality is the product of dirty minds.' (**Alison** *looks at him briefly.*)

Brennan   Uh . . . Ashby. David Ashby. Tory MP for . . .

Toop   Ah ha . . .

Brennan   Leicester . . . no, North West Leicestershire. Yes?

Toop   Yes.

Brennan   Yes!

Toop   Year?

Brennan   Ninety . . . four.

Toop   Bonus point?

Brennan   Go on.

Toop   Wife's name? (*Pause. To* **Alison**.) I think I've got him, darling.

Alison   Well, whoop-dee-doo.

Toop   Come on . . .

Brennan   Syl . . . it begins with an S.

Toop   I'm saying nothing.

Brennan   Sylvia. Definitely Sylvia. (**Toop** *smiles.*) Well?

Toop   Syl-vana!

Brennan   Oh, God, well Sylvia's close enough.

Toop   No way! Ha! Two bonus points to me. (*He tots up the scores on a piece of paper.*) That's seventy-three and a half to you, seventy to me.

Brennan   OK, OK, right . . . who is X in this sentence? OK? 'When Wafic needed a question answered, X would go directly to his mother for an answer.' (*Beat.*)

Toop   Mother . . . who has a mother he would go to. . . ? Oh, wait, of course. Mark Thatcher and Mumsie. It's the Al Yamamah arms deal. Mark made over ten million –

Brennan   Twelve, actually –

Toop   Twelve million smackers out of a deal his mother made with the Saudis on behalf of HMG.

Brennan   Who said investigative journalism was dead?

Toop   God, twelve million. For that useless pillock.

Brennan   It doesn't do to dwell on it.

Toop   No, you're right.

Brennan   Bonus point?

Toop   What's the score? Let's see . . . yes, if I get the bonus point we're level. Right.

Brennan   Right. Who was Wafic, what was his profession and what was his nationality?

Toop   That's three questions.

Brennan   No, it's all one.

Toop   Wafic Said, arms dealer, Syrian. Ha!

Brennan   That was too easy.

Toop   OK, well here's an easy one for you then. Ready?

Brennan   Yes.

Toop   OK. 'Something that I was not aware had happened turned out not to have happened.'

Brennan   *Not* to have happened.

Toop   *Not.* (*Beat.*)

Brennan   Doesn't make sense.

Toop   Well, there's a clue. (**Brennan** *thinks hard.*)

Brennan   It's a Tory, yes?

Toop   Oh yes.

Brennan   What year?

Toop   If I give you any help, it halves the points available.

Brennan   Yes, yes.

Toop   You want the year?

Brennan   Yes.

Toop   OK, '92. (*Beat.*)

Brennan   It's got to be either David Mellor or Matrix Churchill. Yes?

Toop   Any more help and there are *no* points available, and *I* take the lead.

Brennan   All right, God you do go on. It's only a game. (**Alison** *looks up.*) So . . . Mellor, '92. First there was the actress . . . then there was the holiday paid for by the Arab woman. (*Beat.*) No. Give us the quote again.

Toop   'Something that I was not aware had happened turned out not to have happened.' (*Beat.*)

Brennan   It's pure *Alice In Wonderland*, so I guess it must be Matrix Churchill. Yes?

Toop   Yes.

Brennan   Yes!

Toop   Steady on, it's only a game. (*Beat.*) So who said it?

Brennan   Could be anyone . . . Alan Clark, Heseltine, Waldegrave. (*Beat.*) But it's such a stupid sentence. (*Beat.*) Ah! Got it. Of course. John Major.

Toop   Yes. I was only Foreign Secretary and Chancellor of the Exchequer during the relevant period, how the hell should *I* know what was happening?

Brennan   Or *not* happening –

Toop   As the case may be.

Brennan   And he got away with it.

Toop   What can you do?

Brennan   It's not as if there was any sex involved. And what do you expect from democratic government? The truth?

Toop   The what?

Brennan   It's an old word, fallen into disuse.

Toop   Ah yes, the truth. I remember. (**Alison** *stands*.) All right, darling?

Alison   I'm going to powder my nose. (*She goes.*)

Brennan   Everything all right?

Toop   She's got a bee in her bonnet, because . . . thingy's here.

Brennan   Thingy who?

Toop   You know. Thingy I . . . at the Tory Conference.

Brennan   Oh, Bridget Thingy. Well, of course she's here, she's an employee.

Toop   I know. But I didn't know Alison knew who she was. Apparently she's been turning up quite a bit on Daytime TV. Every time you switch on 'Richard and Judy', there's Bridget Thingy sounding off about the Royals or Norma Major's hemline.

Brennan   Nasty. That's enough to put anyone off their tea and biscuits.

Toop   And who was sat right in front of us on the coach for two hours on the way here? (**Brennan** *winces*.)

Brennan   Ouch. (*Beat.*) Beats me why you did it.

Toop   Because it was there?

Brennan   I knew she was putting it about, but I didn't think you'd be daft enough to have a nibble.

Toop   I know. And that's all it was, a nibble. I still don't know how Alison found out.

Brennan   Tory Central Office getting revenge, in my opinion.

Toop   No. I reckon it was someone on the paper.

Brennan   Maybe it was Bridget. (*Beat.*)

Toop   No. It reflects badly on her as well. (*Pause.*) God, it never used to be like this. Ours used to be a happy paper. The odd indiscretion was par for the course. Now, there only has to be so much as a rumour and the place goes into a feeding frenzy. (*Beat.*) And some bastard keeps leaving condoms on my desk.

Brennan   Condoms?

Toop   Yes.

Brennan   That's a bit below the belt.

Toop   Positively third form. It would be nice to think that the Political Editor was considered above such office nonsense.

Brennan   Keep it zipped up next time.

Toop   Next time? I nearly lost my marriage. And I have to account for every minute now. (*Beat.*) It's horrible when something like this happens. It's as if one's life is suddenly covered with a layer of dirt. (*Beat.*)

Brennan   OK. 'What's the big deal? The child's not dead and they're not even English.'

Toop   Eh? (**Brennan** *looks up to where* **Alison** *is coming back.*) Oh, uh, not Sir Nicholas Scott's wife. His secretary. (**Alison** *sits.*) OK, darling?

Alison   No.

Toop   Why, what's the matter?

Alison   Those toilet things are disgusting.

Toop   Isn't there a proper ladies'?

Alison   Apparently not.

Toop   Well, that's not good enough. Senior members of staff and their families ought to merit some degree of comfort. (**Drummond** *comes on.*) Ah, Robert . . .

Drummond   Stephen, there you are. I thought you were going to wait near the house.

Toop   Alison needed to sit down. She has a bad back.

Drummond   OK, no problem.

Toop   Also, she would very much like to use a proper ladies' rest-room if such a thing is available.

Drummond   Of course it is. There's one inside . . .

Alison   Don't worry, I've been now.

Drummond   Well, when you need it again . . .

Alison   Thanks.

Drummond   Stephen, can we. . . ?

Toop   Of course. I won't be long, darling. Peter will look after you, I'm sure.

Brennan   Pleasure. (**Toop** *and* **Drummond** *start to go.*)

Toop   What's it all about, Rob?

Drummond   It's Malcolm's pitch. I'll leave it to him. (*They're gone.*)

Brennan   Well. Fancy a spin round the grounds?

Alison   With *my* back? (*He smiles.*) I'm afraid I'm not as young as I used to be. I'm not as *any*thing as I used to be. (*Beat.*) Sorry.

Brennan   It's OK. (*Beat.*) Shall I get some more champagne?

Alison   Not on *my* account. I hate the damn stuff. Gives me acid. (*Beat.*) You bugger off if you want to. I won't mind.

Brennan   I don't think you really want to be here, do you?

Alison   What a keen young eye you have.

Brennan   What's the problem? (*Beat.*)

Alison   Oh . . . I'm married to a philandering, pompous nitwit whose idea of civilised fun is to play Parliamentary Sleaze Trivia all afternoon. My children have left home. I have no life beyond four walls in Clapham and the odd shopping trip. I have few friends. My last recollection of the person I'm talking to is of giving him a blow-job in the front seat of his BMW. (*Beat.*) I feel old. (*Beat.*)

Brennan   Erm . . . (*Beat.*)

Alison   Oh, don't worry, I knew you'd be embarrassed.

Brennan   No . . .

Alison   There's no need. I won't bring it up again. (*Beat.*)

Brennan   It was very nice . . .

Alison   We were drunk. End of story.

Brennan   But thanks, anyway . . .

Alison   Happy to have been of service.

Brennan   No, I mean it . . . it was really very good.

Alison   Women of a certain age become adept at the art of fellatio. It's because we're too embarrassed to undress. And it makes the fellatee feel important. It's like feeding a baby. (*Beat. He stands and looks around, slightly embarrassed, then begins absent-mindedly practising his golf swing. She looks at him. He notices her watching, smiles and puts his hands in his pockets.*)

Brennan   I've developed a slice . . .

Alison   Really?

Brennan   Yes, I might have to see a swing doctor about it.

Alison   That is so fascinating, I can hardly begin to tell you.

Brennan   That's what Melissa always says. (*Beat.*) Sorry.

Alison It's all right. I know you have a drop-dead gorgeous twenty-year-old live-in girlfriend with a perfect body and teeth like pearls. You told me. You were crying at the time, I remember. (*Beat.*) Did you, er, sort out that little problem?

Brennan Yes.

Alison Oh, good. (*Beat.*) Where is she, anyway?

Brennan Uh, Milan. Work, y'know . . .

Alison What is it she does, again? Advertising, is it?

Brennan No, she's in the music business.

Alison That's right. I knew it was something tarty. (*Beat.*) That wasn't very adult of me, was it?

Brennan No. (*Beat.*)

Alison Where have they dragged Stephen off to?

Brennan Don't know. Some sort of editorial conference, I expect.

Alison Don't they even stop for a wedding?

Brennan Seems not.

Alison I never see him as it is.

Brennan I didn't think that would worry you.

Alison It doesn't worry me. It's just that about the only comfort I have is making Stephen *un*comfortable. Plus, it reaffirms the principle of duty in marriage. It's my duty, after all, to listen to endless streams of parliamentary gossip as if it actually mattered. And it's his to have me before him constantly as a reminder of the two lives he's wasted. (*Beat.*) That poor girl.

Brennan Who?

Alison Yasmin, Tasmin, Tamsin, whatever her name is. The bride.

Brennan Oh, yeah Tamsin.

Alison   Imagine your wedding day having all the spirituality of an Annual General Meeting.

Brennan   I expect she's well used to it.

Alison   And fancy holding the service in a tent.

Brennan   It's standard practice in the States.

Alison   I know, but a marquee is something you put up then take down. It doesn't exactly reek of a sense of permanence.

Brennan   There's no way you'd get this number of people in a church.

Alison   There is one day that every woman banks on from the time she's a little girl. One day when we're allowed to dream the most preposterous dream of all, that somebody loves us and will love us forever. That this holy event somehow promises a lifetime's happiness. Holding it in a marquee is tantamount to saying: OK, the game's up, we all know it's rubbish. Let's get it over with, strike camp and get out of here. (*Beat.*) All this wealth. And it's all so threadbare. (*Beat.*)

Brennan   What was your wedding day like?

Alison   Mine? (*Pause.*) As you'd expect, knowing Stephen, it was very formal. It was the early seventies, so we all looked doubly ridiculous. Stephen had shoulder-length hair and a sort of Jason King moustache. And his tie was about a mile wide. I wore a wide-brimmed hat covered in flowers and my hair came all the way down to my waist. There's a picture of us on the dressing-table, grinning idiotically. I always look at it and wonder who we are and what we're smiling about. Stephen made a very witty speech. Not funny. Witty. The best man was Roger Altham.

Brennan   Really.

Alison   Yes, they were at the BBC together then. And Roger made a very witty speech also. Not funny. Witty. And I talked a lot of nonsense.

Brennan   I'll bet you didn't.

Alison   According to Stephen I did. (*Beat.*) And I believed him. I always believed him. (*Beat.*) The reason he makes such a successful journalist, I think, is because he's a bit of a bully. He seems to believe that people owe him the obligation to tell him all, and if they're not so inclined, he'll jolly well keep at them until they do. Basically, he thinks he knows more and can do everything better than everybody else, and he tells them so. Somebody mentions America, and Stephen points out that he was our man in Washington for nearly five years. There's nothing he doesn't know. Somebody else mentions the money supply, and Stephen brings up his PPE degree. And he's really just a common or garden know-all. I mean, you should watch *Mastermind* with him. It's life or death during the general knowledge round. (*Beat.*) But his kind of knowing isn't knowing at all. There must be some point to knowledge, after all. Surely its acquisition is supposed to . . . improve us. But he's still the emotionally uptight bossy little schoolboy he always was. (*Beat.*)

Brennan   OK, so what *don't* you like about him? (*Pause.*)

Alison   Don't become like him, will you?

Brennan   You think there's a danger of that?

Alison   So long as you're in this job, there's a danger of that. It's osmosis. Go and stand in the bar, which, surprise surprise, is full of journalists, and you can feel them trying to enter your body. Frantic little things, they are, all desperately penetrating one another over the canapés.

Brennan   Can't say as I was aware of it.

Alison   Ah well, it's too late, you're too busy doing some penetrating of your own, I expect.

Brennan   I hope not. What are the signs?

Alison (*beat*)   One: the assumption of self-importance. Simply because you happen to be present at an important event, that doesn't automatically make you important. The event and the people taking part in it are of importance, not you.

Brennan   The media is always part of the event now. Some events wouldn't even take place if we weren't there.

Alison   Most things will happen regardless of whether you're there or not. Imagine what sort of people would only perform if they knew journalists were watching. Sad cretins, I think. And who wants to waste their time reporting the doings of cretins?

Brennan   Hey, I'm a parliamentary correspondent, it's my job. (*Beat.*)

Alison   Two: don't think that because you know a lot of the story, you know it all. Over the years, you'll come to see things from such a detached, privileged place, that your presumption to speak for the man in the street will ring very hollow indeed. You're foot-soldiers for an Empire – the Empire of News – not brave seekers after truth. What you write has already been scanned, edited and agreed before you've even thought it. There is precious little originality in the press, don't believe it's in your sole possession. Three: don't be too categorical in your chastisement of others who abuse their power, since yours is one of the most abused powers in the world. Four: remember that yours isn't the only method of informing people about this disintegrating world we live in. Or that you're uniquely equipped to improve it. The media won't make the world a more civilised place, nor will politics or sport or any of the other things you revere. No, only art and learning can do that, and we know what you think of *them*. Five: don't confuse freedom of the press with freedom of the people. Given the tiny ideological gene pool which currently owns most of the media, I would say the two were definitely not interchangeable. (*Beat.*) Am I old-fashioned? Or just old?

Brennan   Quaint is the word I'd use.

Alison   Oh dear, that means you're not listening to a word I say.

Brennan   Of course I'm listening. That's what I do.

Alison   Don't forget I've been married to a newspaperman for twenty-four years. I know whereof I speak.

Brennan   I know that. (*Beat.*)

Alison   Six: when you come to marry your Melissa, or whichever lucky girl . . . don't neglect her. Don't be like Stephen.

Brennan   I won't. (*Beat.*)

Alison   If I died with my face disfigured, it would be no good asking Stephen to identify the body. (*Pause. She's on the verge of tears.*)

Brennan   I didn't realise . . .

Alison   I'm sorry . . .

Brennan   I didn't know things were so bad. Stephen doesn't really talk about you.

Alison   That's hardly front-page news.

Brennan   I mean he doesn't talk about the marriage.

Alison   It's a thin subject. (*Beat.*) We don't talk. We don't go out. I love the ballet, movies, theatre, but he won't go. Says they're all silly. And he's a hard news man.

Brennan   He's been under a lot of pressure.

Alison   Yes, it must be very trying, meeting a deadline in time to get your leg over with some tart.

Brennan   No. There are a lot of changes going on. There's quite a few people only hanging on by the skin of their teeth.

Alison   Stephen? (*Beat.*)

Brennan   I honestly don't know.

Alison   Does *he* know? (*Beat.*)

Brennan   He may not quite appreciate the scope of some of the changes.

Alison   Thinks he knows it all.

Brennan   He's not the world's greatest office politician. He doesn't listen. (*Beat.*) You know the weekend course we went on? He . . . had quite a rough ride. Did he say?

Alison   No, he was very quiet when he came home. I assumed he'd been doing something he shouldn't again.

Brennan   No, I can vouch for him there. He was in no fit state that weekend. Gutted, is how the sports pages would describe it.

Alison   Well he didn't seem to learn anything from it.

Brennan   No, he didn't. (*Pause.*) The paper's changing direction, y'see, quite radically. And Stephen hasn't quite come to terms yet with the fact that Internews doesn't bend. He thinks his input still carries some weight, when the truth is that every important decision about the paper has been taken months ago. The takeover was part of a long-term business strategy. We're going to be used to try and put one or more of our competitors out of business. Any talk about reviving the values of a great newspaper is just PR. We'll go wherever we're told.

Alison   And you can live with that?

Brennan   It's all there is. Nobody else is any different, really. (*Beat.*) It's going to be tough on some of the guys, the ones who hanker after the old Fleet Street days, El Vino's, all that. The ones who get all misty-eyed over so-and-so who was a great editor, great character, blah blah blah. But I don't seriously believe it was ever any different. It was probably kinder, but so was . . . *every*thing. Somebody always owned the press, and somebody always had an agenda. Internews didn't suddenly *invent* power, they seized it.

Alison   This new direction, I assume it's rightwards.

Brennan   That's a Stephen question.

Alison   Why?

Brennan   It's not a matter of left and right any more. That's the old battlefield. There *is* no left to speak of. There are simply variations of relatively affluent middle-class opinion. Some opinions are kinder than others, but they all begin and end in the same place. And they're all orchestrated from miles away, from a building high in the sky on another continent. (*Beat.*) Stephen . . . his generation . . . they get steamed up about it, as if going backwards into the future was actually an option. But . . . this is how it is, you know? And some of us don't actually want to go backwards. We're busy creating our own memories, dealing with the world as it is, not as we'd like it to be.

Alison   I hadn't realised how out of touch we were. (**Toop** *appears. He walks towards them slowly, deflated and close to tears.*)

Alison   All done? (*Beat.*) Stephen? (*Beat.*)

Toop   Yes, all done.

Brennan   What's the story?

Toop   There is no story. Not one worth printing, anyway.

Alison   Are you all right? (*Beat.*)

Toop   No, not really.

Alison   What happened?

Toop   I don't know. I'm just . . . taking it in. (*To* **Brennan**.) Have they spoken to you?

Brennan   What, today? No.

Toop   That means you're probably safe.

Alison   Safe? From what?

Toop   The sack. Or demotion, if they give you a choice, like they gave me.

Alison   Demotion? You've been demoted?

Toop   I have indeed.

Alison   To what? (*Beat.*)

Toop   Sketch writer.

Alison   But you did that donkey's years ago.

Toop   I know. Apparently, it was the only thing I was halfway decent at, poking harmless fun at MPs. (*Pause.*)

Brennan   Stephen, I'm sorry.

Toop   Why? It's not your fault.

Brennan   I know, but . . . shit. Shit! (*Pause.*)

Alison   Shall we go?

Toop   We can't leave until the buses leave. (*Pause.*) Should I have resigned, do you think? (*Beat.*) Well, it's too late now.

Alison   And who gets your job? (**Toop** *shakes his head and looks down.* **Alison** *looks at* **Brennan**. *He stares back.*) Resign. (*Beat.*) Stephen. (*He looks up.*) Listen to me. They've treated you disgracefully. It's not too late. Go back. Tell them you resign.

Toop   I can't.

Alison   Show some bloody guts. (*Beat.*)

Toop   That damn woman . . .

Alison   Who?

Toop   Thatcher!

Alison   Oh, for God's sake! Don't be so bloody stupid! Move on! (*Beat.*)

Toop   I love the paper. I love my job. And something I've loved and served for years has turned round and stuck a knife in my heart. (**Alison** *stares at him with a mixture of pity and contempt.*)

Alison   If you don't go back and tell them you resign, I'll call a cab to take me back to London now.

Toop   Don't be ridiculous, it's a two-hour drive.

Alison   I don't care what it costs. And when I get home, I'm packing and leaving.

Brennan   Alison . . .

Alison This is none of your business. (*Beat.*) Well? (*Pause.*) Right. Where's the nearest phone? (*She stands.*)

Toop Ali . . .

Alison I mean it. Do you really want to hang around like some superannuated office boy?

Toop No, but –

Alison With no say? Nobody listening? Patronised, humiliated. Knowing that whatever's going on, it doesn't include you. With everyone laughing at you, saying why the hell does he put up with it? Do you *really* want to live my life? (*He looks at her.*) I know it'll be hard. The paper's been your whole life.

Toop Yes . . .

Alison But it can't be any more. (*Beat.*) You have to make a choice.

Toop I suppose I could write my book.

Alison Yes. Work at home. Spend time with me. Go out together. (*Beat.*)

Toop I feel such a failure.

Alison Internews doesn't decide whether you've failed or not. That's up to you. (*Pause.* **Toop** *gets up.*)

Toop I won't be long. (*He goes.*)

Brennan He won't be back.

Alison Don't tell me they shoot anyone who resigns.

Brennan No, he'll be scooted straight out the front door. One of the buses is scheduled to go back to town early.

Alison Even this lot couldn't be that primitive, surely.

Brennan Oh . . . they go in for symbolic gestures in a very big way. It's *pour encourager les autres.*

Alison But it's so . . . crude.

Brennan   It's . . . just how it is. (*Beat.*) I never expected
Stephen to accept the sketch job. I thought he had more . . .
pride.

Alison   What would *you* have done? (*Beat.*)

Brennan   Point taken. (*Beat.*)

Alison   Congratulations on your promotion.

Brennan   You don't mean that.

Alison   I do. I hope you're a big success.

Brennan   Thanks. (*Beat.*) I'm shit-scared as a matter of fact.

Alison   You wouldn't be any good if you weren't.

Brennan   All I know is this is the scariest ride of my life. But
I'd kill to be on it.

Alison   Just remember they throw you off when the ride
ends. If you don't crash first.

Brennan   There are no guarantees.

Alison   Yes, I know, it's just how it is. Let's hope they see
sense one day, before they ruin us all.

Brennan   No chance. There's too much at stake. Nothing
works according to sense any more. It's the market. A whole
new world. (**Drummond** *comes on.*)

Drummond   Alison . . .

Alison   Yes?

Drummond   Stephen's gone round to the front, uh, would
you mind . . .?

Alison   This is really happening.

Drummond   I'd be very grateful for your co-operation.

Alison   Of course. I'm a very co-operative person. (*Beat. She
walks off.* **Drummond** *winks at* **Brennan** *and goes.* **Brennan**
*takes a sip of champagne, then after a moment he starts practising his golf
swing.*)

Fade.

Section Four

The trophy room. **Kirk** *and* **Drummond** *are standing looking towards the door.* **Kirk** *looks at his watch.*

Kirk Come on, you . . . bastard. (*Pause.*)

Drummond I suppose this is what he's like. (*Beat.*)

Kirk Yes, this is what he's like. (*Beat.*) At least he's the last. I'm dying of hunger.

Drummond Shall I get something sent in?

Kirk No. I'll last. (*Beat.*)

Drummond Are you having the steak or the duck? For dinner.

Kirk The duck. (*Beat.*) You?

Drummond Duck. (*Beat.*) He's supposed to be a really good chef.

Kirk Really good? I think that is probably an understatement. I had a meal at his place in Fulham once. Sublime.

Drummond Great. (*Beat.*) I like to do a bit of cooking, you know. When I'm at home.

Kirk Really?

Drummond Yeah. I'm a wizard with a wok. Chinese, Thai, you know.

Kirk Lovely.

Drummond Yeah. (*Beat.*) It's easy these days, you can get all the proper ingredients.

Kirk The free market.

Drummond That's right. Sauces, spices, the works. (*Beat.* **Kirk** *picks up his champagne glass and raises it to his lips as* **Harry**

Rees *comes in. He is casually dressed and has a can of beer in his hand. He raises the can.*)

Rees   Cheers, Kirk. (*They both drink.*)

Kirk   Rees.

Rees   Long time no see.

Kirk   Must be about five years. (*They shake hands.*)

Rees   No, six.

Kirk   Is it that long?

Rees   Yeah. The last time I saw you was at the *What The Papers Say* awards do. I know it's six years because I keep the award in the khazi, so I see it every day. And there it is: Harry Rees, Foreign Correspondent of the Year, 1991.

Kirk   You keep it in the loo.

Rees   Yeah.

Drummond   How original.

Rees   Well, the mantlepiece is already full. (*Beat.*) Who's this, Kirk? Spock?

Kirk   This is Rob Drummond, my deputy.

Rees   Never heard of him. Where'd he spring from?

Kirk   The ranks.

Drummond   Home Affairs.

Rees   Ah. The shallow end. (*Beat.*)

Kirk   Why don't you have a seat, Harry. (**Rees** *sits, putting a foot up on the table.*)

Rees   Sorry I'm not properly dressed, but I only flew in last night. Forgot to pack the penguin suit.

Kirk   I bet you don't have one.

Rees   Yeah, but if I *did* have one, I forgot to pack it, if you know what I mean. I'd hate to think anybody felt I was deliberately doing less than honour to such a glittering occasion.

Kirk You're taking the piss, Harry.

Rees No, you have to enter into the spirit of the thing to really enjoy a corporate gang-bang. Not wearing the appropriate attire is like going to an orgy and screwing your own wife.

Kirk Well, I guess you'd know . . . (**Rees** *smiles*.)

Rees So, you finally got your arse in the editor's chair of a big Sunday.

Kirk Yes.

Rees Congratulations.

Kirk Thanks.

Rees And how's your last paper doing?

Kirk Fit and well. Circulation stable and production costs down.

Rees That's quite an achievement. How do you do it?

Kirk I sack lots of people and produce a paper that people want to buy.

Rees And don't forget the scratchcards.

Kirk And I sometimes create promotions which enhance the breadth of our market standing.

Rees I've got to hand it to you, you really know your business.

Kirk Thanks, praise indeed.

Rees Whether you know anything about newspapers or not is another question. (*Beat. He smiles*.)

Kirk Newspapers *are* my business.

Rees Ah. We're in safe hands, then. (*Pause*.)

Kirk Look, Harry . . .

Rees Guess who I bumped into in Geneva the other week. (*Beat*. **Kirk** *shakes his head*.) Carol. (*Beat*.) *Your* Carol.

Kirk My *ex*-Carol.

Rees   Yeah, ex. (*Beat.*)

Kirk   I haven't seen her . . . in years.

Rees   Not since the divorce?

Kirk   That's right. (*Beat.*)

Rees   Well, she looks terrific.

Kirk   She always did.

Rees   True. (*Beat.*) What grounds was it, the divorce?
(*Beat.*)

Kirk   Adultery.

Rees   Yours?

Kirk   Hers.

Rees   Oh, yeah. Who was it?

Kirk   I don't know.

Rees   You don't know?

Kirk   Harry . . .

Rees   That's a bit remiss.

Kirk   We're not here to discuss my marriage.

Rees   It just strikes me as odd . . .

Kirk   What we're here for . . .

Rees   I mean, if *my* wife was getting it on the side, I think
I'd quite like to know who the bastard was who was giving it
to her.

Kirk   I dare say. But I don't care.

Rees   You mean she wouldn't tell you.

Kirk   I don't care.

Rees   But I'd want to be in the same room as the guy and
look him in the eye and say: you bastard, you fucked my wife.
I'd just want to look into his eyes.

Kirk   I don't.

Rees   Confrontation, Kirk, that's what I'd be looking for.

Kirk   You're sacked, Harry. (*Beat*.)

Rees   Your restraint is awesome.

Kirk   Sometimes. (*Beat*.) Well?

Rees   What?

Kirk   You're sacked.

Rees   Yes. And? (*Beat*.)

Kirk   I imagined you'd be looking for a confrontation.

Rees   And why should that be?

Kirk   Some people do.

Rees   Well, there's a difference between me and other people. I never expected to last six minutes, let alone six months, with you guys in charge.

Kirk   We had to wait six months. We were forced to give certain guarantees.

Rees   Yes, I heard that. Like making hyenas say grace before dinner, in my opinion, but I don't suppose my opinion counts for five-eighths of twelve-sixteenths of fuck all around here any more.

Kirk   That would be pretty accurate, yes.

Rees   That's fine by me.

Kirk   Good.

Rees   Right then. (*Beat*.)

Kirk   Sorry to have brought you halfway round the world just for this.

Rees   No worries, I was due some access to my kids, and it's not as if *I* paid the airfare. Anyway, I love a good wedding. Long as it's not my own.

Kirk   So what are your plans?

Rees   A bit of freelance. A TV documentary.

Kirk   Really?

Rees   Yeah.

Kirk   When are you making that?

Rees   I've done it. It's mostly in the can.

Kirk   You've done it?

Rees   Yeah.

Kirk   While you've been on our payroll?

Rees   I'm allowed. Read my contract.

Kirk   Your old contract became inoperative the day we took over. You're supposed to have signed a new one.

Rees   Heck, you know, I don't think I ever received one. (**Kirk** *looks at* **Drummond**, *who shrugs.*)

Kirk   So you've been working without a contract.

Rees   No, I haven't been working. Not for you, at any rate.

Kirk   But I was told you were researching a big one.

Rees   I was. And I was filming it.

Kirk   Might I ask what it was?

Rees   Sure. I've been investigating media operations in the Far East.

Kirk   Really? That's a big subject.

Rees   Labyrinthine.

Kirk   But I expect you were able to see through to the heart of the thing.

Rees   I think I may have sifted the odd nugget of truth from the silt which big business habitually throws over its tracks, yeah. (*Beat.*)

Kirk   Of course . . . *we* have interests out there.

Rees   That's hardly a secret.

Kirk   Or, to put it another way, we're probably the major player in the Far Eastern market.

Rees   Probably? No two ways about it, Kirk, Internews is king of the slums.

Kirk   So what angle have you taken?

Drummond   I think we can probably guess.

Rees   Yeah?

Drummond   You'll have done what you always do. You'll have decided the point you're going to make, then twisted the facts to fit. You'll have left out any evidence that contradicts your simplistic notion that somebody must be the villain and somebody else the victim, and you'll have set yourself up as judge, jury and executioner. You'll be filmed in a tropical forest somewhere, oozing indignation and compassion, the very model of left-wing outrage, conning the gullible and plucking the heartstrings of the liberal elite. (*Beat.*)

Rees   You know, on the basis that time is too precious to waste, I think I'll take an immediate dislike to you.

Drummond   Answer the point.

Rees   You don't have a point, you just have an attitude.

Drummond   Cop-out.

Rees   No, see, the thing about being a foreign correspondent is you learn to spot a pygmy when you see one.

Drummond   The truth hurts, eh?

Rees   Anyway, you missed out the clincher. My film will probably win an award.

Drummond   Yeah, the bleeding hearts will be queueing up to kiss your arse. And the rest of us, who choose not to believe in global conspiracies, who happen to believe that most governments do a pretty good job, and most of all, who believe in the values of Western democracy . . . we'll watch your naive, one-sided little programme and we won't know whether to laugh or cry. (*Beat.*)

Rees   Internews is capable of beaming fifty channels into every television in every home with a dish. Fifty channels. Twenty-four hours a day. And I make one programme every couple of years. One programme, one hour long. You must be very insecure, Mr Drummond, if that threatens you so very much.

Drummond   But you don't tell the whole story! With you, it's always: government, business, technology, bad. Any old picturesquely poor peasant, good. You wheel out some half-crippled old git who's probably a Communist anyway, and sit there nodding your head while he spoonfeeds you whatever misinformation you're prepared to swallow. It's a joke. You're a fucking joke. (*Beat.*)

Rees   True, my last film featured many 'half-cripples', as you call them. They were half-crippled because they'd been stupid enough to tread on landmines manufactured in this country, planted by soldiers trained by British military personnel. I should have thought your keen journalist's nose would have detected the faintest whiff of a story there.

Drummond   All unproven assertion.

Rees   No. All proven fact. The documents are public. Needless to say, though, all denied. And the denials given prominence and treated as gospel throughout the Internews empire.

Drummond   We were satisfied with the government's version, it's quite simple.

Rees   And fearless defender of freedom that you are, all it takes is a few pin-striped governmental platitudes, and your conscience is satisfied. That's some conscience, Mr Drummond.

Drummond   See? If it comes from government it must be a lie.

Rees   I know your type of journalist. Your relationship with government is one long, sloppy French kiss. You genuflect to power. Whatever our government and its friends say and do is perfectly OK by you, because they're *your* government. You voted for them, and you told your readers to vote for them. They enact legislation that helps your commercial interests run more smoothly. You're all engaged on the same project. It is, needless to say, profoundly undemocratic, but that doesn't bother you, because the ill-effects are always felt somewhere else, by somebody else, in another part of the country, another part of the world. And powerless people have no place in your sort of journalism, do they?

Drummond   Bullshit.

Kirk   Drummond. (*Pause.*) Harry, this programme . . . can you give me some idea of the line you've taken?

Rees   I've been investigating the methods used by Internews to monopolise the market.

Kirk   Specifically?

Rees   Wait and see. I'd hate to spoil it for you. (*Beat.*) But let's just say I have evidence which shows intimidation of elected politicians, support for oppressive regimes in return for special treatment, and business practices which have unfairly driven out competition. Then there's . . . no. You won't be interested in all this stuff. For you, it's a marvellous success story. You're on your way to global domination. Only good can result.

Kirk   Wait here, will you, Harry?

Rees   Glad to. (**Kirk** *goes out.*) Gone for the thumb screws.

Drummond   You've actually been *spying* on the company?

Rees   What a strange word to use. I'm an investigative reporter.

Drummond   But you don't investigate your own company!

Rees   Don't you? (*Beat.*)

Drummond   Do you have *any* loyalty? To *anything*?

Rees   Only the truth.

Drummond   This is the real world, there's no such thing.
(*Beat.*)

Rees   That I should live to hear a journalist say that.

Drummond   Grow up. (*Pause.*)

Rees   A pal of mine, on another one of your papers, was in
Sarajevo in '92, getting bombed day and night courtesy of
the Serbs, when the Fergie toe-sucking affair broke. They
spiked the piece he wrote – too passionate, they said – which
was probably true, but which was also probably the point.
And they made space for a splash on the toe-sucking.

Drummond   Fucking O level time! You never heard of
news value? (*Beat.*) That thing that drops through the letter-
box every morning, it has a price at the top of the front page,
y'know. And people expect something for that price. Telling
them that having bombs lobbed at you is a shitty experience
is about the same as telling them Michael Barrymore's a
poof. We had already gathered that, thank you very much.
(*He laughs, pleased with himself, and pours a glass of champagne.*)

Rees   And tell me . . . just how much *are* you selling the
paper for these days?

Drummond   Sadly, we're engaged in a vicious price war.

Rees   Which you started.

Drummond   Hey, that's business.

Rees   I suppose if people are only shelling out ten pence,
then their expectations are lowered correspondingly.

Drummond   On the contrary. They think they're getting
a bargain. (*Beat.*)

Rees   It occurs to me that if you were ever anywhere near
Sarajevo you'd be one of the bastards doing the shelling.

Drummond   Well I certainly wouldn't be one of the dumb
bastards getting blown to bits down below. (*Beat.*)

Rees   I can't work out whether you're a true believer or just a clever dick.

Drummond   Oh, I believe all right. I believe there are people who want to take the human race into the next century, and there are people who don't.

Rees   Wrong. There are people who don't want to take the human race into a world run for and by vast corporations who have so-called democratic governments safely in their pocket. You're not the only one who believes. I believe you're an aberration. I believe people will one day turn their backs on you. The danger is that you'll actually succeed before that happens. Which effectively means the end of humankind as we understand it, and eventually, the end of the planet.

Drummond   Boy, are you one demented fucker?! How can you believe that shit?

Rees   Because I've seen far too many people whose lives have been blighted by the things you believe in. People disfigured and crippled, broken psychologically, old people, children, helpless, powerless people. (*Beat.*) And I've done the job I signed up for. I've brought their stories to millions of people.

Drummond   Well aren't you the brave little soldier? (*The door opens and* **Bryan Fleming** *strides into the room, talking and taking off his jacket and tie as he does so.* **Kirk** *follows him in.*)

Fleming   Well, stick my arse in a blender. Harry Rees is causing trouble. Again. (*He's rolling up his sleeves.*) Is this *déjà* bloody *vu*, or what?

Rees   Hi, Bry.

Fleming   Bryan to you, fuckface. (*He looks at* **Drummond**.) I think the following may contain material which some viewers might find disturbing.

Drummond   Good.

Fleming   No, I mean fuck off.

Drummond   Oh.

Fleming   This is not for your ears.

Drummond   Sure. Sorry. I'll be outside. (*He goes.*)

Rees   I'm disappointed, Bry.

Fleming   Why?

Rees   I was expecting the old man. I was looking forward to going a few rounds with the old bludger. Instead, he sends me the shit off his shoe.

Fleming   The old man's enjoying a day in the bosom of his family, thanks. And besides, he wouldn't wipe his arse on you.

Rees   That's a relief.

Fleming   So, Kirk tells me you've been moonlighting.

Rees   I never got a contract, Bry.

Fleming   But you've been using our facilities, right?

Rees   So sue me.

Fleming   That's exactly what I'm going to do. I'm going to sue you in every country where you work. I'm going to slap so many writs on this so-called documentary that it'll be fifty years before you're out of a courtroom. I'll sue anybody who even thinks about showing it, so they never touch you again. Boy, I am going to sue you to death. And that's just before breakfast.

Rees   Which will no doubt consist of three Shredded Wheat.

Fleming   Bottom line, Rees: the tiniest fact that doesn't stand up and I'll have your bollocks in a vice.

Rees   Have no fear, Bry. It all stands up.

Fleming   Such as?

Rees   Do you really think I'm going to give you advance warning? Sweat it, Bry. (*Beat.*)

Fleming   OK. We can take it.

Rees   But *can* you? I'd say you've got a bad case of the squits.

Fleming   We can do without bad publicity in that part of the world.

Rees   That's right, because it's not all signed, sealed and delivered yet, is it? There's still a bit of business to be done, a few deals to come to fruition.

Fleming   We're there, mate, no worries. So shit on your programme. Hell, shit on it anyway.

Rees   Thanks, Bry. (*He smiles.*) Why are the curtains closed? It's like you're ashamed of something.

Fleming   You're a queer bugger, Rees.

Rees   No, I'm plug ordinary. You're the strange ones. (*Beat.*) What's it all for? How did news turn into this?

Fleming   Because one man had a vision.

Rees   Right, that's how wars start.

Fleming   It *is* a war, mate.

Rees   And you don't pay a lot of heed to the Geneva Convention.

Fleming   None. No prisoners.

Rees   But why?

Fleming   Because we're proud. Of what we are and of what we've done. We don't give it up easy.

Rees   How can you possibly be proud of what you do, the moral squalor you create? How *can* you be proud of that?

Fleming   We don't create, we supply. We supply information and entertainment, that's all. If a country we're operating in needs a good kick up the arse, we give it one, like we did over here. If some societies are sick, we didn't make them that way. If the people didn't like it, if they were all to switch off, we'd be out of business tomorrow. But they don't.

The little buggers just keep switching on, because they want what we give them.

Rees   But if you're the major supplier, you're all they know. And you've made sure you're the major supplier, one way or another, by busting the competition. So you set the standard, you write the rules. Subscribe or sod off, that's about it.

Fleming   Is it my fault the competition's fucking incompetent?

Rees   It wouldn't matter most of the time if the competition was fucking superhuman, because you've got the muscle and the money to see off just about anybody.

Fleming   Don't forget we've also got the nerve to do things other companies wouldn't even dream.

Rees   You've got to, because every so often something comes along that forces you to act before it gets a slice of the action.

Fleming   You're talking nine quarts of puke here, Rees.

Rees   Yeah? OK. Digital. You've got the analogue market sewn up tight, haven't you, so why should you spend money to go digital and threaten the stranglehold you've already got? Because video on demand is just over the horizon, that's why. A computerised system that offers any film at any time of day, but which can only be delivered by cable, not by satellite. So what can you do? Time for a bit of technology upgrade. You come up with a digital decoder that receives up to five hundred channels. Great, that means even more choice for the masses. But wait, it won't really, because you'll use dozens of channels at a time to show the same movie starting at five- or ten-minute intervals, so it can be watched at virtually any time. And so video on demand has its market taken away. And no new cable is needed, no telephone lines or central computer, none of the expensive stuff. This is dirt cheap.

Fleming   And fucking clever.

Rees   And, on top of that, anybody looking to hire space on a satellite finds that it's all been pre-booked by you. There's choice for you. There's free competition.

Fleming   So in your version we give our competitors a pat on the arse and offer them a slice of something they weren't clever enough to have thought of or dedicated enough to work for? In your dreams, fuckface. We take the risks, we win the prize.

Rees   Is that the only purpose? (*Beat.*) Do you really believe that someone else is going to snatch it all away from you if you stop to reflect for just a second on what your blanket presence does, actually *does* to the societies you take over? Is it really so dangerous for you to face up to your own malevolence?

Fleming   Listen, mate, the old man cares, all right? He's a fucking Christian. He's a family man. He has a moral philosophy, and so does the company. (**Rees** *laughs.*)

Rees   Sorry . . . no, I'm sorry . . . that is just too funny for words.

Fleming   And I'll tell you something *I* believe, OK?

Rees   Go for it.

Fleming   I believe we're the free world's best protection.

Rees   Against what?

Fleming   Against anybody who wants to tell the people what to think, read or watch.

Rees   Anybody other than you, you mean.

Fleming   We offer such an amazing range of choice, there's no reason to go anywhere else. Besides, nobody else can offer what we can.

Rees   Yet.

Fleming   Ever. (*Beat.*)

Rees   That's a very profound moral philosophy.

Fleming   Business leads. The rest follows. We're a neutral agent.

Rees   And shit doesn't stink.

Fleming   Ours doesn't, mate. Ours doesn't. (*He laughs and picks up his jacket and tie, rolls down his sleeves and goes to the door.*) You go ahead with that programme, and I guarantee you we'll squash you flat.

Rees   I'm sure you'll do your best.

Fleming   You might find a lot of countries refusing you a visa. Can't be much of a foreign correspondent if you can't go nowhere. Can you, sport? (*He goes.* **Kirk** *pours a glass of champagne.*)

Kirk   I didn't know you two knew each other.

Rees   He sacked me from the *Sydney Globe* in the seventies. Well, to be fair, he sacked half the workforce. It wasn't personal.

Kirk   He's pretty expert at rationalising businesses.

Rees   Yeah, it's quite an art, sacking people. It must require heaps of selfless dedication.

Kirk   Someone hires, someone fires. The wheels turn. (*Pause.*)

Rees   So what are your plans for the paper?

Kirk   Complete relaunch.

Rees   And how long will that last?

Kirk   Till the novelty wears off. Then we think of something else. (*Beat.*) The fact is, what few people in print will acknowledge yet, is that newspapers are dead. They've gone from cutting edge to obsolete in thirty years, and nobody seems to have quite noticed. Except for the readers, that is. All the trends are down. Having freed ourselves from organised labour and regulation, we should be flying. But there's too much competition now from alternative technologies. Print's share of the market is shrinking fast, and we need to be ready for what comes next.

Rees   Which is?

Kirk   Well, I'd like to see the paper published as a glossy magazine. All the sections inside two covers. Throw out any part of the format that reminds people of a Sunday rag. They've clearly had enough of that.

Rees   You don't think that your relentless drive downmarket might have something to do with that?

Kirk   Negligible . . .

Rees   Oh, come on, that was the Internews strategy, surely. Pollute the market, distort it, drag the quality and the price as low as they can go, and then, if there still *is* a market left after that, fine, because you're the major player, and if there isn't, tough, another outmoded product becomes history, and anyway, you control most of the alternatives.

Kirk   I'm not privy to the company's strategy at that level. (*He smiles.*)

Rees   It's rather like a boxer going into an opponent's dressing-room with some heavies before a fight and working him over, then carrying on with the fight, and winning, naturally, as if he knew nothing about the fact that the other guy came into the ring with a broken nose and no teeth.

Kirk   Markets are unpredictable, you have to do what you can to ensure a level playing field.

Rees   And this relaunch . . . my guess is that the paper's going to be a lot cheaper to produce than before.

Kirk   Well we're hardly going to make it more expensive to produce.

Rees   So, in the long-term, quality will decline and even more people will have become disillusioned with newspapers.

Kirk   You're not hearing me, Harry. There won't even *be* newspapers in the long-term. (*Beat.*) I've had people through here all day, people we're shedding. And for every one of those poor bastards there's another one whose job is safe. For a couple of years. Maybe five. Ten at most. (*Beat.*) If I'm right about newspapers, think what that means for our profession. Gone the same way as coal-miners.

Rees   Where does that leave *you*?

Kirk   Diversifying. Like you, I find television offers the kind of challenges and rewards that stimulate me.

Rees   Thank God. I'd hate to think of you out of a job.

Kirk   No danger of that. (**Rees** *stands. He looks bothered for a moment, then goes to the curtains and draws them back, flooding the room with sunlight.*)

Rees   That's better. (*He goes.* **Kirk** *smiles and finishes his champagne.* **Drummond** *comes in.*)

Drummond   I bet Fleming lit a bloody rocket under his backside, didn't he?

Kirk   Oh, yes.

Drummond   Harry Rees. Piece of crap. You know he came in his own car?

Kirk   No, did he?

Drummond   Yeah. The only one who wouldn't do as he was told. Arsehole.

Kirk   Well. There you go. (**Drummond** *pours them more champagne.*)

Drummond   It's been quite a day.

Kirk   Yes. Quite a success.

Drummond   Right. To the most successful Sunday newspaper in Britain. (*He holds his glass up.*)

Kirk   Aye. (*They clink glasses and drink. There is a knock at the door.*) Come in. (*The* **Waitress** *comes in.*)

Waitress   I was told to clear up in here.

Kirk   Fine. It's all yours. (*The two men eye her up for a moment as she begins clearing the bottles away.*) Right. Duck with green peppercorn sauce. I'm starving. (**Kirk** *and* **Drummond** *go. The* **Waitress** *drains a glass of champagne and notices* **Slater**'*s handbag on the floor beside the chair. She stops for a moment, then swiftly picks up the bag, rummages through it, and takes out all the credit cards and paper money. She stuffs the bag down the side of the chair, lifts her skirt and puts the cards and money into her knickers. Beat. She picks up a tray, fills it with empty bottles and heads for the door.*)

Fade.

End.

Methuen Modern Plays

include work by

Jean Anouilh
John Arden
Margaretta D'Arcy
Peter Barnes
Sebastian Barry
Brendan Behan
Edward Bond
Bertolt Brecht
Howard Brenton
Simon Burke
Jim Cartwright
Caryl Churchill
Noël Coward
Sarah Daniels
Nick Dear
Shelagh Delaney
David Edgar
Dario Fo
Michael Frayn
John Godber
Paul Godfrey
John Guare
Peter Handke
Jonathan Harvey
Iain Heggie
Declan Hughes
Terry Johnson
Barrie Keeffe
Stephen Lowe
Doug Lucie

John McGrath
David Mamet
Patrick Marber
Arthur Miller
Mtwa, Ngema & Simon
Tom Murphy
Phyllis Nagy
Peter Nichols
Joseph O'Connor
Joe Orton
Louise Page
Joe Penhall
Luigi Pirandello
Stephen Poliakoff
Franca Rame
Philip Ridley
Reginald Rose
David Rudkin
Willy Russell
Jean-Paul Sartre
Sam Shepard
Wole Soyinka
C. P. Taylor
Theatre de Complicite
Theatre Workshop
Sue Townsend
Judy Upton
Timberlake Wertenbaker
Victoria Wood

Methuen World Classics *and*
Methuen Contemporary Dramatists

Aeschylus (two volumes)
Jean Anouilh
John Arden (two volumes)
Arden & D'Arcy
Aristophanes (two volumes)
Aristophanes & Menander
Peter Barnes (three volumes)
Sebastian Barry
Brendan Behan
Aphra Behn
Edward Bond (five volumes)
Bertolt Brecht (six volumes)
Howard Brenton (two volumes)
Büchner
Bulgakov
Calderón
Jim Cartwright
Anton Chekhov
Caryl Churchill (two volumes)
Noël Coward (five volumes)
Sarah Daniels (two volumes)
Eduardo De Filippo
David Edgar (three volumes)
Euripides (three volumes)
Dario Fo (two volumes)
Michael Frayn (two volumes)
Max Frisch
Gorky
Harley Granville Barker
   (two volumes)
Peter Handke
Henrik Ibsen (six volumes)
Terry Johnson
Bernard-Marie Koltès

Lorca (three volumes)
David Mamet (three volumes)
Marivaux
Mustapha Matura
David Mercer (two volumes)
Arthur Miller (five volumes)
Anthony Minghella (two volumes)
Molière
Tom Murphy (four volumes)
Musset
Peter Nichols (two volumes)
Clifford Odets
Joe Orton
Philip Osment
Louise Page
A. W. Pinero
Luigi Pirandello
Stephen Poliakoff (two volumes)
Terence Rattigan
Christina Reid
Willy Russell
Ntozake Shange
Sam Shepard (two volumes)
Sophocles (two volumes)
Wole Soyinka
David Storey (two volumes)
August Strindberg (three volumes)
J. M. Synge
Sue Townsend
Ramón del Valle-Inclán
Frank Wedekind
Michael Wilcox
Oscar Wilde

new and forthcoming titles in the Methuen Film series

Beautiful Thing
Jonathan Harvey

The Crucible
Arthur Miller

The English Patient
Anthony Minghella

The Krays
Philip Ridley

Persuasion
Nick Dear after Jane Austen

The Reflecting Skin & The Passion of Darkly Noon
Philip Ridley

Twelfth Night
Trevor Nunn after Shakespeare

For a Complete Catalogue of Methuen Drama titles
write to:

Methuen Drama
Michelin House
81 Fulham Road
London SW3 6RB